Praying with the Family of God

Praying with the Family of God

Selections for Children from
The Book of Common Prayer
Compiled with Introduction and Commentary

by Urban T. Holmes

Winston Press

Acknowledgment is hereby given of permission to reprint portions of *The Proposed Book of Common Prayer.*
Copyright © 1977 by Charles Mortimer Guilbert as Custodian of the Standard Book of Common Prayer. All rights reserved.

© 1979 by Winston Press, Inc.
All rights reserved. No part of this book may be reproduced or used in any form without written permission from Winston Press, Inc.

ISBN: 0-03-049551-2
Library of Congress Catalog Card Number: 78-50423

Book design: Maria Mazzara·Schade
Illustrations: Johannes Sprangers

Photographs: Jim LaVigne (page 18), Michael Paul (page 52, 132), Cyril A. Reilly (page 88), Jim L. Bowman (page 170), John D. Firestone and Associates, Inc. (page 156).

Winston Press, Inc., 430 Oak Grove, Minneapolis, MN 55403

5 4 3 2 1

Contents

A Preface for Parents, Teachers, and Priests	vi
Introduction for the Young Reader	viii
Holy Baptism	3
Holy Eucharist	27
Special Days	75
Daily Morning Prayer	117
Daily Prayers for Individuals and Families	167
Glossary	174

A Preface for Parents, Teachers, and Priests

This prayer book is designed to help children participate in the services of *The Book of Common Prayer*. *Praying with the Family of God* includes liturgical material selected from the adult prayer book. There are no changes in language other than simplifications of the rubrics for the benefit of young readers. Sometimes the components in the text of the service are rearranged. For example, optional prayers are incorporated into the main body of the text for easier use.

The selections from *The Book of Common Prayer* have been made on the basis of several criteria. First, the contemporary English services have been chosen because they are the most easily understood. Second, the services selected are those most likely to include children and also those most basic for learning about our Christian beliefs. In some cases certain occasional prayers and a few rubrics which are more appropriate for the celebrant have been omitted for simplicity.

Explanatory material, written to assist children in understanding a part of the worship service, is interspersed with the excerpts from *The Book of Common Prayer*. The excerpted material is always indented.

A story introduces each service in this prayer book. The story illustrates a theme related to the service that follows. Each story tells something of the continuing story of God's relationship with human beings. A commentary follows, providing concrete explanations of how the service reenacts the story's theme. Illustrations supplement the explanations in the text.

Praying with the Family of God has a special objective. As children's liturgies become more popular and adults become more aware of the worship needs of children, we still find ourselves wanting to keep a place for children in our regular church services. To avoid segregating our children, we look for ways to enhance our sense of family by including them. This book is designed to make the achievement of this goal possible. The commentary encourages young readers to think about worship theologically and yet in terms that make sense to them. What develops is a story theology. Moving concretely, as children's minds do, the commentary and the stories attempt to look at the words and actions that compose our worship experiences and to unravel and simplify these elements for young worshipers. In so doing, their own worship experience can be made more vital and enriching.

Read through this book with the children who will use it. You may find it personally helpful. Like children's sermons, which are often more useful to adults than the sermons intended for adults, perhaps this book will be a catalyst for further discussion. In this way, many in the family of God who are no longer children may come to understand the meaning of our worship and to participate in it more fully.

Introduction for the Young Reader

We all know what it's like to sit in church, trying not to squirm, daydreaming about yesterday or tomorrow, gazing at the backs of other people's heads. We try to listen, but sometimes we don't understand the words that are being spoken. We can't even ask questions about what we don't understand because everyone wants us to be quiet. When we open the prayer book, we still may not be able to find the right place, or we may not be able to follow along—or to move back and forth in the book—to keep up with the service.

We also know what it's like to feel exactly the opposite. When we're watching a favorite television show, we follow along excitedly. We may have seen it before. We may even know exactly what's going to happen and when it's going to happen. But we sit there anyway, loving it, waiting for the next familiar event in the story. We've already seen it, but somehow that makes it even better. We can't wait to see it again.

If you've ever been in a play at school, you know the feeling of excitement that comes when you're a part of the story. Not only does the story itself get to be familiar, but you yourself are *in* it. You belong to it. Being a part of it makes it better than just watching.

Going to church and being part of the worship service can feel good and exciting too. For in church a story is being told, a story that you're a part of. It's a real story, and it's a happy story too.

Each of the services in this book is from *The Book of Common Prayer*—the book that stays in the pews of your church. Each service is a different way of telling the story of Jesus and his place in our lives. It is a happy story because it tells us that God cares for us and that he forgives us when we make mistakes. The story tells how his son died and rose again for us, and how, in the end, this resurrection saves us. This story becomes our own story when we go to church.

This book has been written to help you better understand each of the services included here. Instead of just watching, you can really be *in* the story. This book also has some history in it for you. History is the story behind the story—the part that tells you how the story first started. The people of God have been worshiping for thousands of years, and the history of that worship helps us understand what we see in church today.

This book contains explanations written especially for you. They are printed in a wider line than the words from *The Book of Common Prayer.*

Holy Baptism

Jimmy raced out the front door and slammed it behind him. BLAM! He ran down the walk toward the park. It was Saturday morning, the sky was blue—no sign of rain. He ran faster. He was off to play baseball, and he couldn't wait to get started! His parents had given him a new bat for his tenth birthday. Here was his first chance to try it out.

Coming to the corner, Jimmy swirled the bat around his head. It was a great day! He could almost feel himself hitting that first ball as he held the bat tight in his hands. Then, suddenly the bat slipped . . . and . . . CRASH! The bat had sailed out of his hands, through the air, and right into the plate glass window of Harmon's Drug Store.

Disaster! Jimmy stared at the awful hole in the window. He wished he were somewhere else. Everyone on the block came running. Jimmy couldn't move. He just stood there staring at the drug store window display with its bottles and boxes and thousands of tiny pieces of glass. And lying in the middle of it all—his brand new bat. He knew that people were all around him, but he could not look up.

Then he heard one gruff voice above all the others. Somebody was standing right next to him. "Hey kid," the voice said, "who's going to pay for this?" Jimmy didn't know what to say. He kept staring at the ground.

"Did you hear me, kid?" the voice said more harshly this time. "Who's going to take care of this? Answer me that!"

Jimmy opened his mouth to speak, but nothing came out.

Then, just when all the sounds around him were getting jumbled up together, Jimmy heard a voice he knew.

"Jimmy is mine." It was his dad. Jimmy looked up to see his father standing there next to him.

"I'll pay for it," his dad said, putting his hand on Jimmy's shoulder.

You are going to see a Baptism. As you watch, think about Jimmy and his father. In this story Jimmy makes a mistake—a mistake he can't fix by himself, a mistake that can cause him a lot of trouble. But he is not alone. He is part of a family. His father loves him and helps him.

When we come to church, we are with other people who belong to our church family. Our church family is part of the whole family of Christians all over the world.

Members of our Christian family know that each of us belongs to God's family. God is our loving parent—he helps us and cares for us. Our membership in his family begins when we are baptized, when God says to us "You are mine. You belong to my family."

Belonging to God's family means receiving God's help, like Jimmy got help from his father. When we are part of God's family, we know that even when we make mistakes we will still be forgiven. Jimmy's father paid for the broken window. He made it possible for Jimmy's mistake to be fixed. Belonging to God's family is something like that.

We're like Jimmy. Sometimes we make mistakes. When we hurt somebody's feelings, or when we forget a promise we made, or when we don't finish an important task that we started, we know we've made a mistake. We feel sorry when we think it over, and we promise ourselves that we will try to do better next time. We also ask God to forgive us, to trust us to try to do better. We can ask this because we are members of his family. We belong to him like Jimmy belongs to his father.

In baptism God offers to help us be friends with him and with each other. We feel his love; we welcome it. We accept God's help. We are beginning a new life in the family of God.

It is a wonderful thing to be baptized! Think what baptism will mean to the person you will see baptized today.

Baptisms usually happen at the beginning of the Sunday service. This is the time when the Christian family gets together to give thanks to God. When a baptism is celebrated, a new member is joining the family of God. We have most baptisms on Sunday so that the new member can be with others who share a life as members of God's family.

Jimmy never forgot the day his father stood with him in front of the broken window. In fact, every once in a while Jimmy would say to his dad, "Remember when you told the drug store man that I belonged to you and that you would pay for what I did?" Then his father would smile and give Jimmy a hug. Every time he remembered that day, Jimmy felt lucky he had a father. Remembering made him feel stronger.

In our worship, members of God's family are remembering their father and feeling thankful that they belong to him. Just like Jimmy, when they remember, they feel stronger.

What Happens at Holy Baptism

The Beginning
The Collect of the Day
The Lessons
The Sermon
Presenting and Examining the Candidates
The Baptismal Covenant
Prayers for the Candidates
Thanksgiving over the Water
The Baptism
The Ending

The Beginning

A hymn, psalm or anthem may be sung. When the Baptism is part of the Sunday worship service, the celebrant and the people begin the service by reading a few sentences back and forth. These opening words remind us that because of our one baptism, we are members of God's one family.

As the people stand, the Celebrant says

          Blessed be God: Father, Son, and Holy Spirit.
People   And blessed be his kingdom, now and for ever. Amen.

In place of the above, from Easter Day through the Day of Pentecost

Celebrant   Alleluia. Christ is risen.
People   The Lord is risen indeed. Alleluia.

In Lent and on other penitential occasions

Celebrant   Bless the Lord who forgives all our sins;
People   His mercy endures for ever.

The Celebrant then continues

          There is one Body and one Spirit;
People   There is one hope in God's call to us;
Celebrant   One Lord, one Faith, one Baptism;
People   One God and Father of all.
Celebrant   The Lord be with you.
People   And also with you.
Celebrant   Let us pray.

The Collect of the Day

The celebrant reads a special prayer that has been chosen for this particular Sunday in the church year. This prayer is called the *collect*. If the Baptism occurs on a day other than Sunday or another feast day, the Collect is chosen especially for the Baptism. After the Collect is read, the people respond *Amen.*

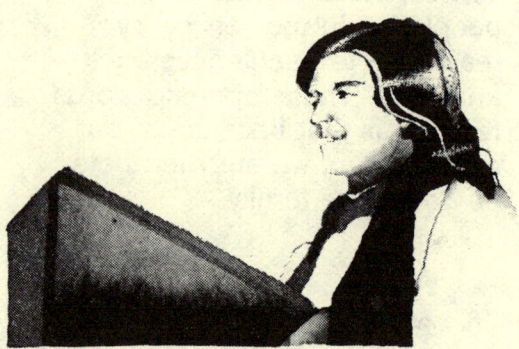

The Lessons

The lessons are read by one or more people who have been chosen to do this. Someday you may be asked to read the lessons.

The people sit. One or two selected Lessons are read, the Reader first saying
    A Reading (Lesson) from _____.

A citation giving chapter and verse may be added.

After each Reading, the Reader may say
    The Word of the Lord.
People   Thanks be to God.

or the Reader may say
    Here ends the Reading (Epistle).

Silence may follow.

A psalm, hymn, or anthem may follow each Reading.

8   Praying with the Family of God

Then, all standing, the Deacon or a Priest reads the Gospel, first saying

>The Holy Gospel of our Lord Jesus Christ according to _____.

People Glory to you, Lord Christ.

After the Gospel, the Reader says

>The Gospel of the Lord.

People Praise to you, Lord Christ.

The Sermon

The sermon may be preached now or after the Peace.

Presenting and Examining the Candidates

The Celebrant says

>The Candidate(s) for Holy Baptism will now be presented.

The early Church baptized only adults who had made the decision to follow Jesus. But as the Church grew, Christian men and women married each other and began to have families. When a child was born, the parents wanted to baptize their new baby. So over the years Baptism became a ceremony for welcoming babies, as well as older people, to the family of God.

When a child is going to be baptized, the parents choose godparents for the child. The godparents, who are already members of God's family, will help the growing child know God's love and care by their example. In this new family the child will receive the special gift of God's grace.

Adults and Older Children

The candidates who are able to answer for themselves are presented individually by their Sponsors, as follows.

Sponsor   I present N. to receive the Sacrament of Baptism.

The Celebrant asks each candidate when presented
　　　　Do you desire to be baptized?
Candidate   I do.

Infants and Younger Children

Then the candidates unable to answer for themselves are presented individually by their Parents and Godparents, as follows.

Parents and Godparents

I present N. to receive the Sacrament of Baptism.

When all have been presented the Celebrant asks the parents and godparents

Will you be responsible for seeing that the child you present is brought up in the Christian faith and life?

Parents and Godparents
I will, with God's help.

Celebrant

Will you by your prayers and witness help this child to grow into the full stature of Christ?

Parents and Godparents
I will, with God's help.

A Christian is a person who follows the example of Jesus and tries to live within the love and acceptance of God's family. Six questions in the baptismal service ask the person being baptized to promise to act like a Christian. The first three questions ask the candidate, with God's help, to avoid experiences that separate us from God's love. The last three questions ask the candidate to follow what leads to grace and love.

Long ago when only adults were baptized, they faced west as they answered questions like the first three of these. They did this because the people of that time thought that the west stood for the forces that are against God. Then, when they promised to follow Jesus, they turned and faced east, the direction that stood for God. This is why the fourth question begins "Do you *turn* to Jesus Christ. . . ." (We still see signs of this belief today. In *The Wizard of Oz* the wicked witches are from the west and east, and the good witches are from the north and south.)

Then the Celebrant asks the following questions of the candidates who can speak for themselves, and of the parents and godparents who speak for the infants and the younger children.

Question	Do you renounce Satan and all the spiritual forces of wickedness that rebel against God?
Answer	I renounce them.
Question	Do you renounce the evil powers of this world which corrupt and destroy the creatures of God?
Answer	I renounce them.
Question	Do you renounce all sinful desires that draw you from the love of God?
Answer	I renounce them.
Question	Do you turn to Jesus Christ and accept him as your Savior?
Answer	I do.

Question Do you put your whole trust in his grace and love?
Answer I do.
Question Do you promise to follow and obey him as your Lord?
Answer I do.

After all have been presented, the Celebrant addresses the congregation, saying

Will you who witness these vows do all in your power to support *these persons* in *their* life in Christ?
People We will.

After the questions have been answered, the celebrant asks everybody in the congregation to help the new members. When the people answer "We will," they are promising to give love and care to the new member of the family of God. Their answer shows that members of a family help each other.

The Celebrant then says these or similar words

Let us join with *those* who *are* committing *themselves* to Christ and renew our own baptismal covenant.

The Baptismal Covenant

When we see someone being baptized, we think about the meaning of our own baptism. We remember this meaning by stating our Christian beliefs out loud and together. A statement of our beliefs is called a *creed*. We say it now to help us remember and share what we believe.

In our creed we answer three questions. When we answer the first question, we are saying we believe that God made us. When we answer the second question, we are saying we believe that God sent his son to us to show us how to live and to make it possible for us to live that way too. When we answer the third question, we are saying we believe that the Holy Spirit gives us the power to be practicing and believing Christians. This answer is sometimes called *the doctrine of the Trinity.*

Then we answer more questions. We promise we will try, with God's help, to be good members of God's family, to fight against evil, to tell our friends about Jesus, to take care of each other, and to make the world a place where people can live in fairness and peace and freedom, as God wants them to live. All these answers together are our *Baptismal Covenant.* This covenant is the promise we make, to each other and to God, to live and act as Christians.

Celebrant   Do you believe in God the Father?
People   I believe in God, the Father almighty, creator of heaven and earth.

Celebrant   Do you believe in Jesus Christ, the Son of God?

People	I believe in Jesus Christ, his only Son, our Lord.
	    He was conceived by the power
	        of the Holy Spirit
	        and born of the Virgin Mary.
	    He suffered under Pontius Pilate,
	        was crucified, died, and was buried.
	    He descended to the dead.
	    On the third day he rose again.
	    He ascended into heaven,
	        and is seated at the right hand
	        of the Father.
	    He will come again to judge the
	        living and the dead.

Celebrant	Do you believe in God the Holy Spirit?

People	I believe in the Holy Spirit,
	    the holy catholic Church,
	    the communion of saints,
	    the forgiveness of sins,
	    the resurrection of the body,
	    and the life everlasting.

Celebrant	Will you continue in the apostles' teaching and fellowship, in the breaking of bread, and in the prayers?
People	I will, with God's help.
Celebrant	Will you persevere in resisting evil, and, whenever you fall into sin, repent and return to the Lord?
People	I will, with God's help.
Celebrant	Will you proclaim by word and example the Good News of God in Christ?
People	I will, with God's help.
Celebrant	Will you seek and serve Christ in all persons, loving your neighbor as yourself?

People   I will, with God's help.

Celebrant   Will you strive for justice and peace among all people, and respect the dignity of every human being?

People   I will, with God's help.

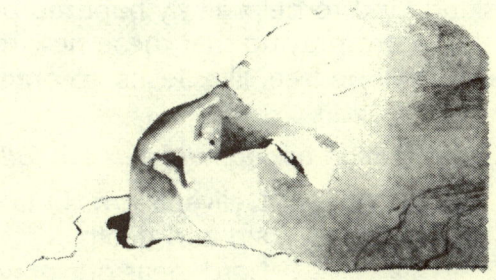

Prayers for the Candidates

The Celebrant says to the congregation

Let us now pray for *these persons* who *are* to receive the Sacrament of new birth [and for those (this person) who *have* renewed *their* commitment to Christ.]

Now we ask for God's help for those who are going to be baptized. Each of these small prayers asks God to help the baptized person, in some particular way, to live a full Christian life.

The celebrant calls Baptism the sacrament of new birth. When we are born, we become members of the *human family*. When we are baptized, we begin a new life as a member of *God's family*. This is why we say that baptism is the sacrament that brings new birth.

Baptism   15

These prayers also mention death, not the physical death which happens in the human family, but a spiritual death which happens in God's family. This spiritual death occurs when we are cut off from God, when we are separated from what is good. This kind of death leaves us alone, like Jimmy in our story before he heard his father say "Jimmy is mine." Sometimes this death describes the way we feel when we are cut off from God, cut off from our Christian family. In these prayers we are asking God to help newly baptized people in their new life. We are praying that these new members of God's family will be free, like Jesus, to enter into a new life.

A Person appointed leads the following petitions.

Leader   Deliver *them,* O Lord, from the way of sin and death.
People   Lord, hear our prayer.

Leader   Open *their hearts* to your grace and truth.
People   Lord, hear our prayer.

Leader   Fill *them* with your holy and life-giving Spirit.
People   Lord, hear our prayer.

Leader   Keep *them* in the faith and communion of your holy Church.
People   Lord, hear our prayer.

Leader   Teach *them* to love others in the power of the Spirit.
People   Lord, hear our prayer.

Leader   Send *them* into the world in witness to your love.
People   Lord, hear our prayer.

Leader   Bring *them* to the fullness of your peace and glory.
People   Lord, hear our prayer.

The Celebrant says

Grant, O Lord, that all who are baptized into the death of Jesus Christ your Son may live in the power of his resurrection and look for him to come again in glory; who lives and reigns now and for ever. *Amen.*

Thanksgiving over the Water

We gather around the baptismal font. The font contains the water that will be used for the Baptism. The celebrant says a prayer, remembering some of the special ways that water has helped human beings be close to God from the beginning of life. Water is also part of our own daily lives—we drink it, we wash in it, we swim in it. All living things need water to survive. We use water in a baptism ceremony to remind ourselves of the new life that baptism brings to us. At the end of the Thanksgiving Prayer, we ask God to bless this water so that we can use it for the special purpose of bringing new members into God's family.

We are now ready for the Baptism. As you watch, think about how a Baptism reminds us of what happened to Jesus. When Jesus died, he found new life. When we are baptized, we begin a new life too, as members of God's family.

The Celebrant blesses the water, first saying

	The Lord be with you.
People	And also with you.
Celebrant	Let us give thanks to the Lord our God.
People	It is right to give him thanks and praise.

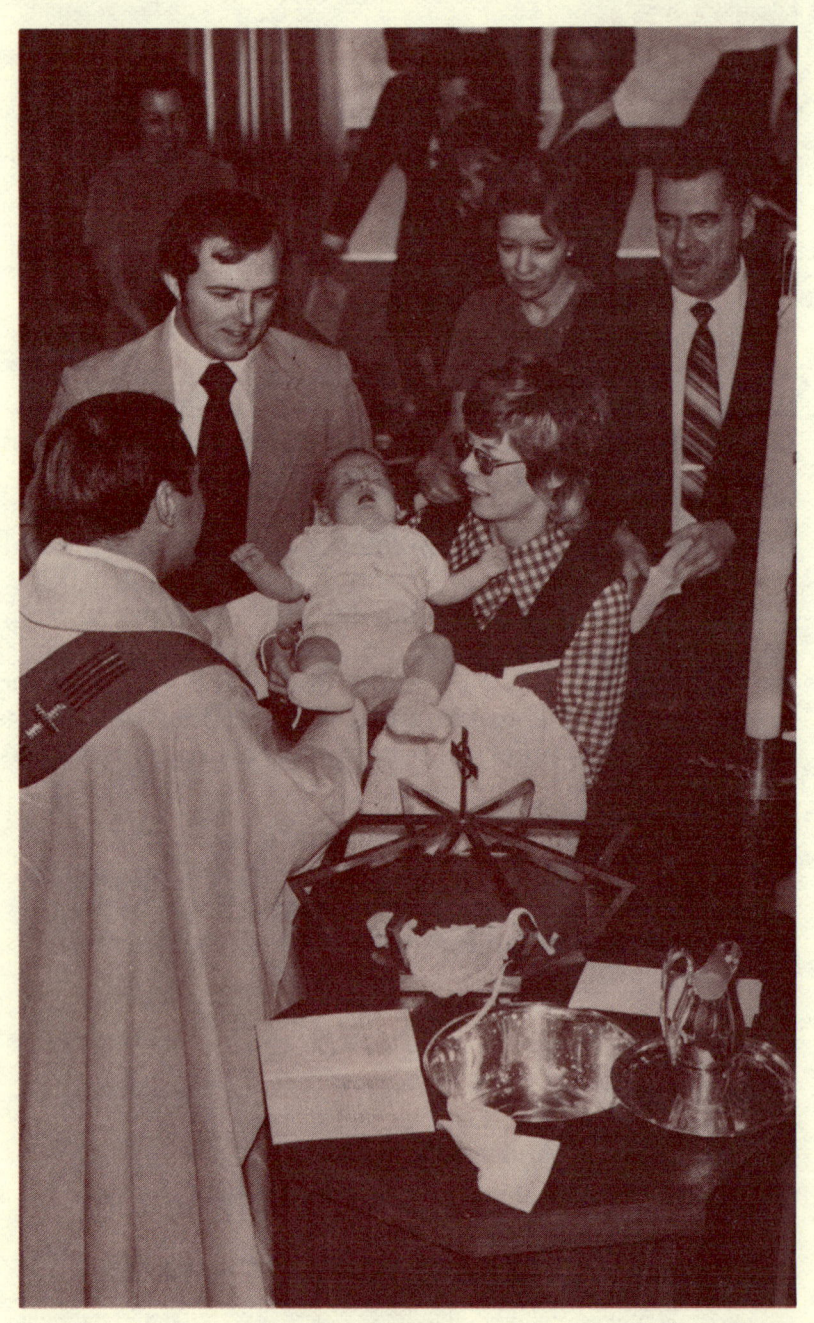

Celebrant

We thank you, Almighty God, for the gift of water. Over it the Holy Spirit moved in the beginning of creation. Through it you led the children of Israel out of their bondage in Egypt into the land of promise. In it your Son Jesus received the baptism of John and was anointed by the Holy Spirit as the Messiah, the Christ, to lead us, through his death and resurrection, from the bondage of sin into everlasting life.

We thank you, Father, for the water of Baptism. In it we are buried with Christ in his death. By it we share in his resurrection. Through it we are reborn by the Holy Spirit. Therefore in joyful obedience to your Son, we bring into his fellowship those who come to him in faith, baptizing them in the Name of the Father, and of the Son, and of the Holy Spirit.

At the following words, the Celebrant touches the water.

Now sanctify this water, we pray you, by the power of your Holy Spirit, that those who here are cleansed from sin and born again may continue for ever in the risen life of Jesus Christ our Savior.

To him, to you, and to the Holy Spirit, be all honor and glory, now and for ever. *Amen.*

The Baptism

In the Episcopal church, people are usually baptized by having a little water poured over their heads. Sometimes, but not often, they actually get into the water. Both actions have the same meaning—the baptized person is joining God's family. And both actions come from the same tradition—the public bath.

In the lives of early Christians, the public bath was an important and daily habit. The baths were like small swimming or wading pools, and many people bathed in them together. When they finished, they rubbed on a sweet-smelling oil, just like people today sometimes put on lotion or perfume after a bath. The actions we see at a Baptism—pouring on water and then rubbing on oil—come from this tradition that has gone on for hundreds of years.

Each part of the Baptism has special meaning. It is an outward sign of what is happening when people are baptized. As they go under the water, they leave behind the loneliness of being separated from God. When they come up out of the water, washed clean, they enter the family of God. Then, they are marked with the *chrism,* which shows that they are surrounded by God's love—they are special to him.

The word *chrism* comes from the Greek word *chrisma,* which means *to anoint.* Chrism is often a mixture of olive oil and the sweet-smelling gum from a tree. Since the beginning of the Church, chrism has been used to anoint people for special purposes.

Praying with the Family of God

As we watch a Baptism, we think about what is happening at this moment. Each action stands for the mystery that we can't see as this baptized person joins the family of God. Once and for all, God is saying "Jimmy is mine."

Each candidate is presented by name to the Celebrant, or to an assisting priest or deacon, who then immerses, or pours water upon, the candidate, saying

N., I baptize you in the Name of the Father, and of the Son, and of the Holy Spirit. *Amen.*

When this action has been completed for all candidates, the Bishop or Priest, at a place in full sight of the congregation, prays over them, saying

Let us pray.

Heavenly Father, we thank you that by water and the Holy Spirit you have bestowed upon *these* your *servants* the forgiveness of sin, and have raised *them* to the new life of grace. Sustain *them,* O Lord, in your Holy Spirit. Give *them* an inquiring and discerning heart, the courage to will and to persevere, a spirit to know and to love you, and the gift of joy and wonder in all your works. *Amen.*

Then the Bishop or Priest places a hand on the person's head, marking on the forehead the sign of the cross [using Chrism if desired] and saying to each one

N., you are sealed by the Holy Spirit in Baptism and marked as Christ's own for ever. *Amen.*

Or this action may be done immediately after the administration of the water and before the prayer above.

Baptism   21

The Ending

When all have been baptized, the Celebrant says
Let us welcome the newly baptized.

Celebrant and People
We receive you into the household of God. Confess the faith of Christ crucified, proclaim his resurrection, and share with us in his eternal priesthood.

If Confirmation, Reception, or the Reaffirmation of Baptismal Vows is not to follow, the Peace is now exchanged.

Celebrant   The peace of the Lord be always with you.
People   And also with you.

A wonderful thing has just happened! Someone has just become a part of the family of God. The celebrant asks the people gathered around the font to welcome the baptized person as a new member of the family.

Then, as families often do, we show our love by greeting the people near us with welcoming and caring words.

We can also share a hug or a handshake to show how we feel about these other members of our Christian family.

The baptism service usually ends at this point, and we continue with the worship service. Sometimes when the bishop is there, we have a short service in which young adults and grown-ups *renew their baptismal promise to follow Jesus.* They do this when they understand the meaning of their baptism better than they did when they were younger. The renewal is a way of showing that they now have a fuller understanding of what it means to be a Christian.

The Holy Eucharist

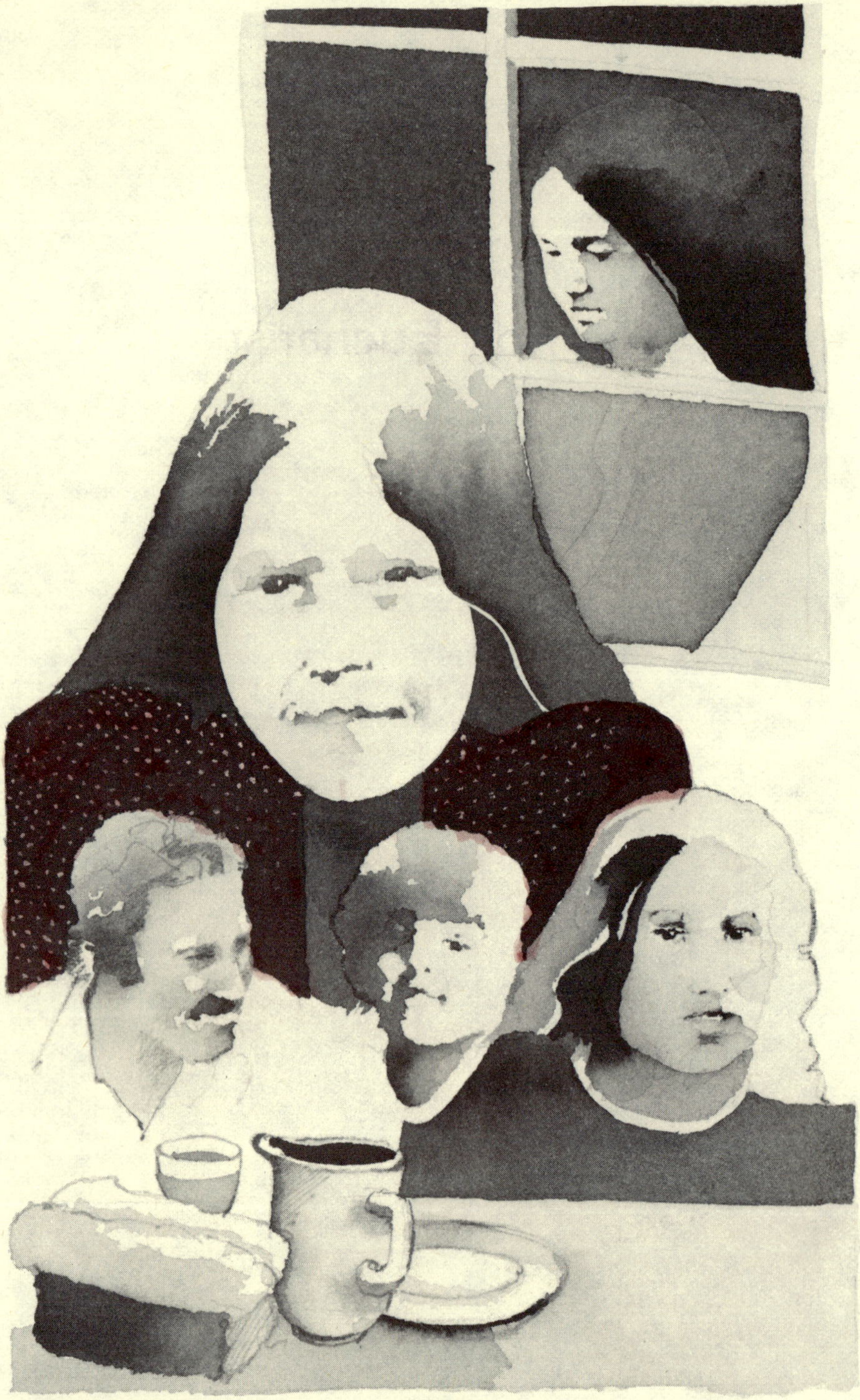

The turkey was delicious. "This is the best Thanksgiving dinner *ever*," Tim said to his older sister Kathy. He was already planning to take a second helping of the corn bread dressing. "Maybe this tastes so good," said Kathy, "because it's a special Thanksgiving."

Last year at this time Kathy was sick. She came to the table for Thanksgiving dinner, but she only stayed a few minutes. After that, a long time went by when Tim hardly ever saw Kathy playing. She seemed to spend almost all of her time in her room, and when she was up, she looked tired.

Tim began to wonder what was going on. Then in early spring Tim's mom spoke to him about it. "You know, Tim," she said, "Kathy has been sick for quite a while now." Tim listened as his mother tried to explain. "Inside of us we have something called *kidneys*. We have two of them, and they work like filters—keeping our blood clean by filtering out things that could hurt us." Tim thought he understood that, so his mother continued. "Kathy's kidneys don't work anymore. She needs to go to the hospital every week so that a machine can clean her blood. If she couldn't use that machine, she might die."

The rest of the spring and early summer were very confusing around Tim's house. Kathy spent a lot of time either resting or at the hospital. Then late last summer Tim's dad announced that his mother and Kathy were soon going into the hospital. He sat down with Tim and told him why.

"If Kathy had just one good kidney, instead of two sick ones, she wouldn't need that machine, and maybe she could be well again. Even though we are born with two kidneys, we can live with one if it's healthy. So your mother is going to have an operation which will take out one of her kidneys, and then the doctors will operate on

Kathy and give your mother's kidney to her. Then we hope both of them will be able to live, each with one good kidney."

It sounded complicated to Tim. He could tell that everybody in his family was a little scared.

After the operation, two weeks went by before Tim's mom came home from the hospital. Soon afterward Kathy came home too. At first Kathy lay on the couch all day, but then she started moving around and even playing outside a little. After a while everybody began to feel better. Life around the house began to be more like it was before Kathy got sick.

So now it was Thanksgiving again. Early this morning Tim's dad had said "This Thanksgiving we really have a lot to celebrate." Tim thought about that as he sat down at the table. His aunt and uncle were there, and the parish priest and his wife were guests also. Everyone was quiet for the blessing. Then, before they began, Tim's father talked a little about how much God had done for them in helping Kathy get well. After that, Father Reynolds led everyone in the blessing.

While it was still quiet, Father Reynolds turned to Kathy. "You know," he said, "we must all give thanks for your mother. She gave up part of her body, and by doing that, she gave you back your life."

The Sunday service is often called the Holy Eucharist. The word *eucharist* means *thanksgiving*. The service is a meal during which we give thanks. Tim's special thanksgiving dinner is a little like the Holy Eucharist—the special meal at which we thank Jesus because he gave us back our lives by giving up his own.

In our story, Tim's mom made a sacrifice so that Kathy could live. But Tim's mom didn't die, she got well. Imagine how much *more* Jesus gave. Jesus gave everything so that we ourselves could have new life. This is why we celebrate and show thankfulness.

Do you remember how good the turkey and dressing tasted to Tim? Many people think the bread and wine at the Eucharist taste good too. The wine may tickle a bit when you swallow it, and sometimes it will make your mouth pucker. The wine has a sharp taste—it almost seems to be alive! The good taste of the bread and wine make us glad to be alive and thankful to Jesus, who gives us life.

The service of the Holy Eucharist has two parts. During the first part, called *The Word of God,* we talk about what Jesus did for us when he died. When Tim's father talks about Kathy getting well and all that God had done for them, his words are a little like the first part of the Eucharist.

During the second part, called *The Holy Communion,* we eat the bread and drink the wine. When Tim and his family ate the turkey and the dressing, their meal was a little like Holy Communion. When we eat the bread and wine in the Eucharist, Jesus is there with us. We are as close to him as we can be.

What Happens at Holy Eucharist

The Word of God
    The Beginning
    A Song of Praise
    The Collect
    The Lessons
    The Gospel
    The Sermon
    The Nicene Creed
    The Prayers of the People (Forms I-VI)
    Confession of Sin
    The Peace

The Holy Communion
    The Offertory
    The Great Thanksgiving—Eucharistic Prayers
    The Lord's Prayer
    The Breaking of the Bread
    The Eating and Drinking
    The Ending

The Word of God

The Beginning

The service may begin with the singing of a hymn, psalm, or anthem. Then the priest greets us and we reply. This is like somebody saying "Good morning" or "Isn't it good to be here?" and someone else answering back "Good morning to *you*" or "It certainly is!" We have three different ways to say the opening greeting. We use the first one most of the time. We use the second one at Easter, when we are especially happy for the resurrection of Jesus. We use the third one when we are especially sorry for our sins.

The people standing, the Celebrant says

          Blessed be God: Father, Son, and Holy Spirit.

People   And blessed be his kingdom, now and for ever. Amen.

In place of the above, from Easter Day through the Day of Pentecost

Celebrant   Alleluia. Christ is risen.
People   The Lord is risen indeed. Alleluia.

In Lent and on other penitential occasions

Celebrant   Bless the Lord who forgives all our sins;
People   His mercy endures for ever.

After our greeting we sometimes say a prayer asking God to help us think about him during this worship service.

The Celebrant may say
Almighty God, to you all hearts are open, all desires known, and from you no secrets are hid: Cleanse the thoughts of our hearts by the inspiration of your Holy Spirit, that we may perfectly love you, and worthily magnify your holy Name; through Christ our Lord. *Amen.*

A Song of Praise

We begin our thanksgiving meal by saying or singing a song of praise. The three songs in the prayer book are very old—about 1600 years old, in fact. We can even sing one of them, the *kyrie eleison,* in Greek, the language it was first sung in long ago. Or we can choose to sing a song that isn't from the prayer book.

Everyone stands.

Glory to God in the highest,
    and peace to his people on earth.

Lord God, heavenly King,
almighty God and Father,
    we worship you,
    we give you thanks,
    we praise you for your glory.

Lord Jesus Christ, only Son of the Father,
Lord God, Lamb of God,
you take away the sin of the world:
    have mercy on us;
you are seated at the right hand of the Father:
    receive our prayer.

For you alone are the Holy One,
you alone are the Lord,
you alone are the Most High,

Jesus Christ,
   with the Holy Spirit,
   in the glory of God the Father. Amen.

On other occasions the following is used.

Lord, have mercy.
Christ, have mercy.
Lord, have mercy.

or this

Kyrie eleison.
Christe eleison.
Kyrie eleison.

or this

Holy God,
Holy and Mighty,
Holy Immortal One,
Have mercy upon us.

The Collect of the Day

So far we have been getting ready to hear the Word of God. We finish our preparation by saying a prayer called a *collect*. It has this name because in this prayer we "collect"—or sum up—some of our most important thoughts and tell God about them. The collect changes every Sunday of the year, and sometimes it changes on weekdays. Listen carefully to the special thought for today.

The Celebrant says to the people
             The Lord be with you.
People   And also with you.
Celebrant Let us pray.

The Celebrant says the Collect.

People   Amen.

Holy Eucharist   33

The Lessons

Now we're ready to hear the story of God and his people as it is told in the Bible. There are two or three readings for each service, and these readings change every week. You can go to church every Sunday for three years and never hear the same reading twice. Each set of readings tells us about one main idea, one important way that God gives us *new life.* As you listen to these readings, try putting that one main idea in your own words. Think about what the reading tells you about the new life that God gives us.

The people sit. One or two selected Lessons are read, the Reader first saying

A Reading (Lesson) from _____.

A citation giving chapter and verse may be added. After each Reading, the Reader may say

       The Word of the Lord.

People   Thanks be to God.

or the Reader may say

       Here ends the Reading (Epistle).

Silence may follow.

A psalm, hymn, or anthem may follow each Reading.

The Gospel

The last reading is the most important one. It is called the Gospel because it always comes from one of the four Gospels of the New Testament: Matthew, Mark, Luke, or John.

Then, all standing, the Deacon or a Priest reads the Gospel, first saying

           The Holy Gospel of our Lord Jesus Christ according to _____

People   Glory to you, Lord Christ.

After the Gospel, the Reader says

           The Gospel of the Lord.

People   Praise to you, Lord Christ.

The Sermon

The sermon helps us understand what we've just heard read from the Bible. Since the Bible was written a long time ago, we need the sermon to help us apply the Bible's teachings to our own times and our own communities.

The word *sermon* means a *talk* or *conversation,* and that is exactly what it is. The sermon is written by the priest or by someone that the priest has asked to preach in his or her place. In many churches there is a special place for preaching called the *pulpit.* The Gospel is often read from the same place.

There are many different styles of sermons. Some are very emotional, some are very simple and informative, and still others are casual and conversational. The style of the sermon depends on the personality of the speaker, on the subject of the sermon, and on the season of the church year. For example, a sermon at Christmas is likely to be different than one during Lent.

The Nicene Creed

First we heard readings from the Bible, and then in the sermon we heard how these readings apply to our lives today. Now we all stand up together as members of the family of God and say out loud what we believe. A statement of our belief is called a *creed.* This particular creed, called the Nicene Creed, was written in the city of Nicea, where Turkey is now, over 1600 years ago. The Bible readings and the sermon gave us many little examples or ideas about the story of God and humans. Now we say the *whole idea* out loud, in only a few words. The Nicene Creed tells the most important parts of the story of God's love for his people.

On Sundays and other Major Feasts everyone stands to say

We believe in one God,
   the Father, the Almighty,
   maker of heaven and earth,
   of all that is, seen and unseen.

We believe in one Lord, Jesus Christ,
   the only Son of God,
   eternally begotten of the Father,
   God from God, Light from Light,
   true God from true God,
   begotten, not made,
   of one Being with the Father.
   Through him all things were made.
   For us and for our salvation
      he came down from heaven:
   by the power of the Holy Spirit
      he became incarnate from the Virgin Mary,
      and was made man.

For our sake he was crucified under
    Pontius Pilate;
he suffered death and was buried.
On the third day he rose again
    in accordance with the Scriptures;
he ascended into heaven
    and is seated at the right hand of the Father.
He will come again in glory to judge the living
    and the dead,
    and his kingdom will have no end.

We believe in the Holy Spirit, the Lord, the giver
    of life,
who proceeds from the Father and the Son.
With the Father and the Son he is worshiped
    and glorified.
He has spoken through the Prophets.
We believe in one holy catholic and apostolic
    Church.
We acknowledge one baptism for the
    forgiveness of sins.
We look for the resurrection of the dead,
    and the life of the world to come. Amen.

The Prayers of the People

A long time ago, there was the custom for some people to get up and leave church just before the Nicene Creed was said. The people who left were people who hadn't been baptized or people who didn't believe the Creed. All the people who remained in church were baptized Christians, who then stated their beliefs out loud in the Creed. These people were called The Faithful. The Prayers of the People are also called the Prayers of the Faithful or the Prayers of the People of God. In these prayers we share our concerns and hopes with God.

Here are six different prayer forms for us to use. In most of them, there is a place for us to respond after the celebrant begins the prayer. In some of them, there is a time for silence, when we can say our own prayers. Each prayer asks for the same things, so the difference in each form has to do with what words we use to respond, how often we respond, and how long we pray.

These prayers are offered for the church and its members and missions, for the nation and those in authority, for the welfare of the world, for the community, for people in trouble, and for the dead. A saint may be remembered when appropriate. Changes or additions may also be made to suit the occasion.

The celebrant may introduce these prayers with an invitation suited to the occasion or the season, or with the Proper of the Day.

A bar in the margin means the petition may be left out. In these and other responsive prayers, the words in italics are spoken by the people.

Prayers of the People (Form I)

Form I is based on prayers used in the liturgies of the church in Greece and Syria over 1000 years ago. When we use this form today, we can think of our common faith with Christians who lived long ago and far away.

Deacon or other leader
With all our heart and with all our mind, let us pray to the Lord, saying, "Lord, have mercy."

For the peace from above, for the loving kindness of God, and for the salvation of our souls, let us pray to the Lord.
Lord, have mercy.

For the peace of the world, for the welfare of the holy Church of God, and for the unity of all peoples, let us pray to the Lord.
Lord, have mercy.

For our Bishop, and for all the clergy and people, let us pray to the Lord.
Lord, have mercy.

For our President, for the leaders of the nations, and for all in authority, let us pray to the Lord.
Lord, have mercy.

For this city (town, village, _____), for every city and community, and for those who live in them, let us pray to the Lord.
Lord, have mercy.

For seasonable weather, and for an abundance of the fruits of the earth, let us pray to the Lord.
Lord, have mercy.

For the good earth which God has given us, and for the wisdom and will to conserve it, let us pray to the Lord.
Lord, have mercy.

For those who travel on land, on water, or in the air [or through outer space], let us pray to the Lord.
Lord, have mercy.

For the aged and infirm, for the widowed and orphans, and for the sick and the suffering, let us pray to the Lord.
Lord, have mercy.

For _____ , let us pray to the Lord.
Lord, have mercy.

For the poor and the oppressed, for the unemployed and the destitute, for prisoners and captives, and for all who remember and care for them, let us pray to the Lord.
Lord, have mercy.

For all who have died in the hope of the resurrection, and for all the departed, let us pray to the Lord.
Lord, have mercy.

For deliverance from all danger, violence, oppression, and degradation, let us pray to the Lord.
Lord, have mercy.

For the absolution and remission of our sins and offenses, let us pray to the Lord.
Lord, have mercy.

That we may end our lives in faith and hope, without suffering and without reproach, let us pray to the Lord.
Lord, have mercy.

Defend us, deliver us, and in thy compassion protect us, O Lord, by thy grace.
Lord, have mercy.

In the communion of [_____ and of all the] saints, let us commend ourselves, and one another, and all our life, to Christ our God.
To thee, O Lord our God.

Silence

The Celebrant adds a concluding Collect.

Prayers of the People (Form II)

Form II was written by an Episcopal priest, the Reverend Alfred Shands, for a congregation in our nation's capital, Washington, D.C. When he wrote it, he was thinking of the people who make our government work.

In the course of the silence after each bidding, the People offer their own prayers, either silently or aloud.

I ask your prayers for God's people throughout the world; for our Bishop(s) _____ ; for this gathering; and for all ministers and people.
Pray for the Church.

Silence

I ask your prayers for peace; for goodwill among nations; and for the well-being of all people.
Pray for justice and peace.

Silence

I ask your prayers for the poor, the sick, the hungry, the oppressed, and those in prison.
Pray for those in any need or trouble.

Silence

I ask your prayers for all who seek God, or a deeper knowledge of him.
Pray that they may find and be found by him.

Silence

I ask your prayers for the departed [especially _____].
Pray for those who have died.

Silence

> *Members of the congregation may ask the prayers or the thanksgivings of those present*

I ask your prayers for _____ .
I ask your thanksgiving for _____ .

Silence

Praise God for those in every generation in whom Christ has been honored [_____ whom we remember today].
Pray that we may have grace to glorify Christ in our own day.

Silence

The Celebrant adds a concluding Collect.

Prayers of the People (Form III)

Form III comes from the Anglican church in New Zealand, a country on the other side of the world. This prayer reminds us of the common faith we share with fellow-Anglicans around the world.

> *The Leader and People pray responsively*

Father, we pray for your holy Catholic Church;
That we all may be one.
Grant that every member of the Church may truly and humbly serve you;
That your Name may be glorified by all people.
We pray for all bishops, priests, and deacons;
That they may be faithful ministers of your Word and Sacraments.
We pray for all who govern and hold authority in the nations of the world;
That there may be justice and peace on the earth.

Give us grace to do your will in all that we undertake;
That our works may find favor in your sight.

Have compassion on those who suffer from any grief or trouble;
That they may be delivered from their distress.

Give to the departed eternal rest;
Let light perpetual shine upon them.

We praise you for your saints who have entered into joy;
May we also come to share in your heavenly kingdom.

Let us pray for our own needs and those of others.

Silence

The People may add their own petitions.

The Celebrant adds a concluding Collect.

Prayers of the People (Form IV)

Form IV is also from the Anglican church. It was first written in England, was changed for the church in South Africa, and then we adopted it in the United States.

Deacon or other leader
Let us pray for the Church and for the world.

Grant, Almighty God, that all who confess your Name may be united in your truth, live together in your love, and reveal your glory in the world.

Silence

Lord, in your mercy
Hear our prayer.

Holy Eucharist 43

Guide the people of this land, and of all the nations, in the ways of justice and peace; that we may honor one another and serve the common good.

Silence

Lord, in your mercy
Hear our prayer.

Give us all a reverence for the earth as your own creation, that we may use its resources rightly in the service of others and to your honor and glory.

Silence

Lord, in your mercy
Hear our prayer.

Bless all whose lives are closely linked with ours, and grant that we may serve Christ in them, and love one another as he loves us.

Silence

Lord, in your mercy
Hear our prayer.

Comfort and heal all those who suffer in body, mind, or spirit; give them courage and hope in their troubles, and bring them the joy of your salvation.

Silence

Lord, in your mercy
Hear our prayer.

We commend to your mercy all who have died, that your will for them may be fulfilled; and we pray that we may share with all your saints in your eternal kingdom.

Silence

Lord, in your mercy
Hear our prayer.

The Celebrant adds a concluding Collect.

Prayers of the People (Form V)

Form V, like Form I, comes from the Eastern church, which includes churches in Greece, Asia Minor, the Balkans, and Russia. Unlike Form I, it is a modern prayer.

Deacon or other leader

In peace, let us pray to the Lord, saying, "Lord, have mercy" (*or* "Kyrie eleison").

For the holy Church of God, that it may be filled with truth and love, and be found without fault at the day of your coming, we pray to you, O Lord.

Here and after every petition the People respond

Kyrie eleison.
or
Lord, have mercy.

For N. our Presiding Bishop, for N. (N.) our own bishop(s), for all bishops and other ministers, and for all the holy people of God, we pray to you, O Lord.

For all who fear God and believe in you, Lord Christ, that our divisions may cease, and that all may be one as you and the Father are one, we pray to you, O Lord.

For the mission of the Church, that in faithful witness it may preach the Gospel to the ends of the earth, we pray to you, O Lord.

For those who do not yet believe, and for those who have lost their faith, that they may receive the light of the Gospel, we pray to you, O Lord.

For the peace of the world, that a spirit of respect and forbearance may grow among nations and people, we pray to you, O Lord.

For those in positions of public trust [especially _____], that they may serve justice, and promote the dignity and freedom of every person, we pray to you, O Lord.

For all who live and work in this community [especially_____], we pray to you, O Lord.

For a blessing upon all human labor, and for the right use of the riches of creation, that the world may be freed from poverty, famine, and disaster, we pray to you, O Lord.

For the poor, the persecuted, the sick, and all who suffer; for refugees, prisoners, and all who are in danger; that they may be relieved and protected, we pray to you, O Lord.

For this *congregation* [for those who are present, and for those who are absent], that we may be delivered from hardness of heart, and show forth your glory in all that we do, we pray to you, O Lord.

For our enemies and those who wish us harm; and for all whom we have injured or offended, we pray to you, O Lord.

For ourselves; for the forgiveness of our sins, and for the grace of the Holy Spirit to amend our lives, we pray to you, O Lord.

For all who have commended themselves to our prayers; for our families, friends, and neighbors; that being freed from anxiety, they may live in joy, peace, and health, we pray to you, O Lord.

For _____ , we pray to you, O Lord.

For all who have died in the communion of your Church, and those whose faith is known to you alone, that, with all the saints, they may have rest in that place where there is no pain or grief, but life eternal, we pray to you, O Lord.

Rejoicing in the fellowship of [the ever-blessed Virgin Mary, *(blessed N.)* and] all the saints, let us commend ourselves, and one another, and all our life to Christ our God.
To you, O Lord our God.
Silence

The Celebrant adds a concluding Collect, or the following Doxology

For yours is the majesty, O Father, Son, and Holy Spirit; yours is the kingdom and the power and the glory, now and for ever. *Amen.*

Prayers of the People (Form VI)

Form VI was written by an Episcopal priest, the Reverend Carroll Simcox. The responses of the people are quotations from the Bible.

The Leader and People pray responsively

In peace, we pray to you, Lord God.
Silence

For all people in their daily life and work;
For our families, friends, and neighbors, and for those who are alone.

For this community, the nation, and the world;
For all who work for justice, freedom, and peace.

For the just and proper use of your creation;
For the victims of hunger, fear, injustice, and oppression.

For all who are in danger, sorrow, or any kind of trouble;
For those who minister to the sick, the friendless, and the needy.

For the peace and unity of the Church of God;
For all who proclaim the Gospel, and all who seek the Truth.

For [N. our Presiding Bishop, and N. (N.) our Bishop(s); and for] all bishops and other ministers;
For all who serve God in his Church.

For the special needs and concerns of this congregation.

Silence

The People may add their own petitions.

Hear us, Lord;
For your mercy is great.

We thank you, Lord, for all the blessings of this life.

Silence

The People may add their own thanksgivings.

We will exalt you, O God our King;
And praise your Name for ever and ever.

We pray for all who have died, that they may have a place in your eternal kingdom.

Silence

The People may add their own petitions.

Lord, let your loving-kindness be upon them;
Who put their trust in you.

We pray to you also for the forgiveness of our sins.

Silence may be kept.

Leader and People

Have mercy upon us, most merciful Father;
in your compassion forgive us our sins,
known and unknown,
things done and left undone;

and so uphold us by your Spirit
that we may live and serve you
   in newness of life,
to the honor and glory of your Name;
through Jesus Christ our Lord. Amen.

The Celebrant ends with an absolution or a suitable Collect.

Confession of Sin

We have just thanked God and shared some of our needs with him. Now we say a prayer to remind ourselves, in a general way, that we have all made mistakes while we have tried to be loving persons. We know that Jesus' love is total. Although we try to follow his example, we will always fall short of it. During this prayer we look at our own failings, and we remind ourselves that we need to keep trying to love better. We are all human, and we are all imperfect. But we can look at our imperfections and remind ourselves of Jesus' perfect love for us. We can say we're sorry—both for the things we did and for the things we didn't do. We're sorry that our love hasn't been as complete as Jesus' love—not as deep and not as fair.

This prayer will mean something different for each of us, because we each limit our love differently. But the words are about something we have in common: We all want to love as perfectly as Jesus, and we all feel sadness when we see that we have loved less. As we say we're sorry, we are reminding ourselves that this love we try to show is the same love that Jesus has for each of us.

The Deacon or Celebrant says

Let us confess our sins against God and our neighbor.

Silence may be kept.

Minister and People

Most merciful God,
we confess that we have sinned
   against you
in thought, word, and deed,
by what we have done,
and by what we have left undone.
We have not loved you with our
   whole heart;
we have not loved our neighbors
   as ourselves.
We are truly sorry
   and we humbly repent.
For the sake of your Son Jesus Christ,
have mercy on us and forgive us;
that we may delight in your will,
and walk in your ways,
   to the glory of your Name.

Amen.

The Bishop when present, or the Priest, stands and says

Almighty God have mercy on you, forgive you all your sins through our Lord Jesus Christ, strengthen you in all goodness, and by the power of the Holy Spirit keep you in eternal life. *Amen.*

The Peace

The first of the two parts of the Eucharist ends with "the peace." The peace is the love which only God can give, which unites us to him and to one another. We know God gives us his peace because of what we have heard in the Bible, what we have talked about in the sermon, the answer he gives to our prayers, and the belief that he forgives us when we confess our sins. The family of God now shares its knowledge of the peace with words and, in many parishes, with some action. Long ago this was called the "kiss of peace," because it was customary for people to exchange a kiss at this time. The custom in your parish may be to give a warm handshake or a hug and to say something like "The peace of the Lord be always with you." As you do this, keep in mind that it is the peace that God gives in Jesus that we are sharing with one another.

All stand. The Celebrant says to the people
          The peace of the Lord be always with you.
People   And also with you.

Then the Ministers and People may greet one another in the name of the Lord.

The Holy Communion

Our thanksgiving meal begins now. Everything we've done so far has been to get us ready for Holy Communion, for when we eat bread and drink wine together. Jesus first showed us how to do this, and he promised that he would be present whenever we share this special meal.

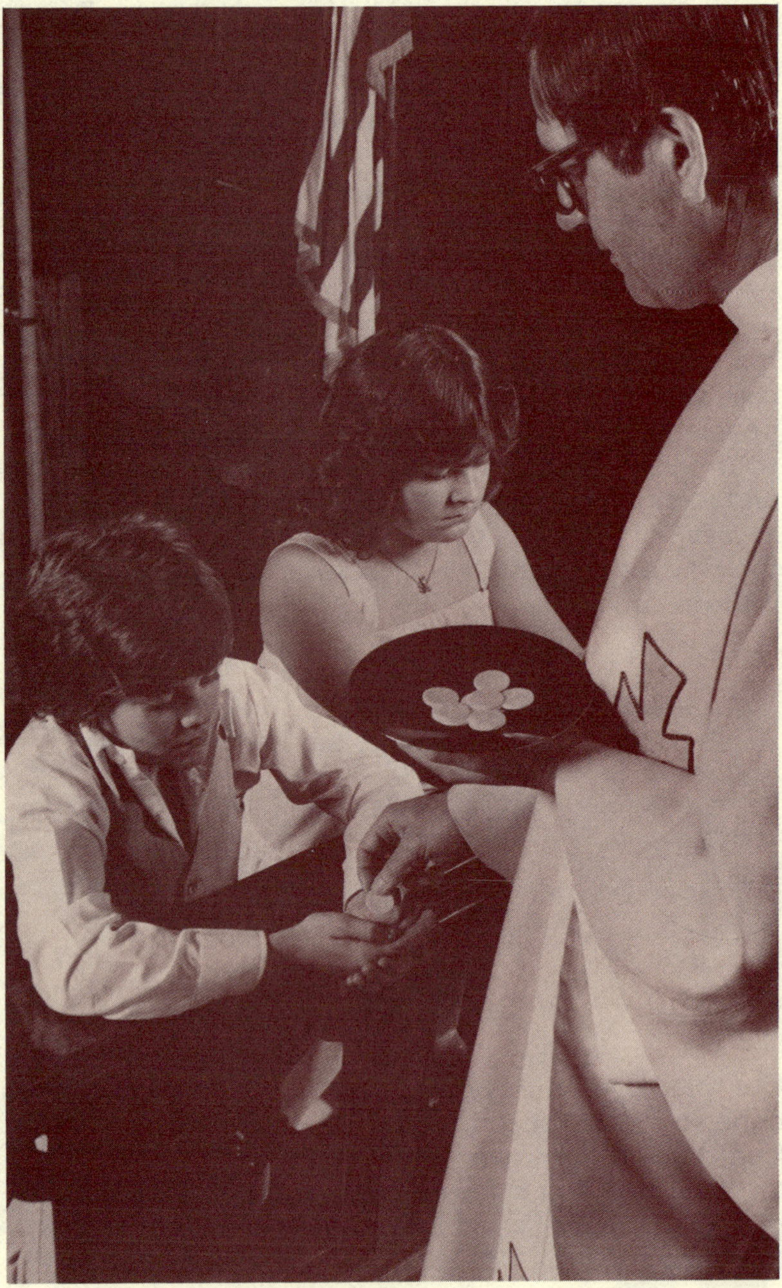

The word *communion* reminds us of other words: *community, common, communicate, commune.* These are all from the Greek word *koinōnia,* which was one name for Christians in the New Testament. We gather together for Holy Communion at the Lord's table because we are the Lord's community.

The Offertory

During this first part of the Holy Communion, the Offertory, we *offer* our bread and our wine to God. These are our gifts, and we are giving them to God and to all people. It's as if we're saying "Here, God, take these gifts so that they can bring life to all people." This is also the time that money is sometimes collected in order to provide support for the church and for the people it helps.

In our story, Kathy's mom risks her life to help her daughter. Her gift reminds us of the meaning of the Offertory. In another story, from the Bible, a boy gives Jesus five loaves of bread and two fish, and Jesus makes that food into enough to feed five thousand people. You can read this story in the Gospel of John 6:1-13. Both of these stories remind us of the meaning of the Offertory. It is a time of gift-giving, a time when we give part of ourselves for the sake of someone else.

The Great Thanksgiving—Eucharistic Prayers

In the Offertory we remember that this is a moment when we're doing something *for someone else's sake.* In the Great Thanksgiving we are asking a blessing, like Tim's father did in the story. The prayers we say during this part of Holy Communion are called the Eucharistic Prayers. Although each of the four forms of these prayers is slightly different, they have some things in common.

They all start with the same words, and they all tell the history of what God has done for us, especially on the night of the Last Supper. They tell many details about that important night. In all the prayers, the priest asks the Holy Spirit to make the bread and wine holy, as the body and blood of Jesus. This is what we mean when we say that the priest asks God to *consecrate* the bread and wine.

We believe that as we eat the bread and drink the wine we are experiencing the story of the resurrection as if we are really there. Then we're able to share in the new life that Jesus brings to us by his dying and rising again.

When we hear the words *Holy, Holy, Holy,* we remember that much of what we're doing comes from Jewish tradition and that Christianity grew out of Judaism. They are the words of Isaiah the prophet, in Isaiah 6:3.

The differences in the Prayers of Thanksgiving are somewhat like the differences in the Prayers of the People. They all say the same thing in different ways and, therefore, can be used to suit different occasions and different feelings.

Eucharistic Prayer A

Eucharistic Prayer A was written by the Reverend H. Boone Porter. It uses images from the early church to emphasize what Jesus did for us by suffering, dying, and being raised from the grave. We use this prayer often during Lent and Easter, because that's a time in the church year when we concentrate on these events in Jesus' life.

The people remain standing. The Celebrant, whether bishop or priest, faces them and sings or says
                The Lord be with you.
People   And also with you.

Celebrant	Lift up your hearts.
People	We lift them to the Lord.
Celebrant	Let us give thanks to the Lord our God.
People	It is right to give him thanks and praise.

Then, facing the Holy Table, the Celebrant continues

It is right, and a good and joyful thing, always and everywhere to give thanks to you, Father Almighty, Creator of heaven and earth.

Here a Proper Preface is sung or said on all Sundays, and on other occasions as selected.

Therefore we praise you, joining our voices with Angels and Archangels and with all the company of heaven, who for ever sing this hymn to proclaim the glory of your Name:

Celebrant and People

Holy, holy, holy Lord,
    God of power and might,
heaven and earth are full of your glory.
    Hosanna in the highest.
Blessed is he who comes in the
    name of the Lord.
    Hosanna in the highest.

The people stand or kneel.

Then the Celebrant continues

Holy and gracious Father: In your infinite love you made us for yourself; and, when we had fallen into sin and become subject to evil and death, you, in your mercy, sent Jesus Christ, your only and eternal Son, to share our human nature, to live and die as one of us, to reconcile us to you, the God and Father of all.

He stretched out his arms upon the cross, and offered himself, in obedience to your will, a perfect sacrifice for the whole world.

As the words about the bread are spoken, the Celebrant holds the bread or places a hand on it; and at the words about the cup, the Celebrant holds the cup or places a hand on it and on any other container holding wine that will be consecrated.

On the night he was handed over to suffering and death, our Lord Jesus Christ took bread; and when he had given thanks to you, he broke it, and gave it to his disciples, and said, "Take, eat: This is my Body, which is given for you. Do this for the remembrance of me."

After supper he took the cup of wine; and when he had given thanks, he gave it to them, and said, "Drink this, all of you: This is my Blood of the new Covenant, which is shed for you and for many for the forgiveness of sins. Whenever you drink it, do this for the remembrance of me."

Therefore we proclaim the mystery of faith:

Celebrant and People

Christ has died.
Christ is risen.
Christ will come again.

The Celebrant continues

We celebrate the memorial of our redemption, O Father, in this sacrifice of praise and thanksgiving. Recalling his death, resurrection, and ascension, we offer you these gifts.

Sanctify them by your Holy Spirit to be for your people the Body and Blood of your Son, the holy food and drink of new and unending life in him.

Sanctify us also that we may faithfully receive this holy Sacrament, and serve you in unity, constancy, and peace; and at the last day bring us with all your saints into the joy of your eternal kingdom.

All this we ask through your Son Jesus Christ. By him, and with him, and in him, in the unity of the Holy Spirit all honor and glory is yours, Almighty Father, now and for ever. *Amen.*

Eucharistic Prayer B

Eucharistic Prayer B has a different emphasis than Prayer A. Like all the other prayers, it speaks of what Jesus sacrificed for us. Unlike the others, this prayer describes how God became man in Jesus, and how we will be together with God at some time in the future. This prayer fits the Advent, Christmas, and Epiphany seasons.

The people remain standing. The Celebrant, whether bishop or priest, faces them and sings or says

           The Lord be with you.
People   And also with you.
Celebrant Lift up your hearts.
People   We lift them to the Lord.
Celebrant Let us give thanks to the Lord our God.
People   It is right to give him thanks and praise.

Then, facing the altar, the Celebrant proceeds

It is right, and a good and joyful thing, always and everywhere to give thanks to you, Father Almighty, Creator of heaven and earth.

Here a Proper Preface is sung or said on all Sundays, and on other occasions as appointed.

Therefore we praise you, joining our voices with Angels and Archangels and with all the company of heaven, who for ever sing this hymn to proclaim the glory of your Name:

Holy Eucharist

Celebrant and People

Holy, holy, holy Lord,
> God of power and might,
heaven and earth are full of your glory.
> Hosanna in the highest.
Blessed is he who comes in the name
> of the Lord.
> Hosanna in the highest.

The people stand or kneel.
Then the Celebrant continues

We give thanks to you, O God, for the goodness and love which you have made known to us in creation; in the calling of Israel to be your people; in your Word spoken through the prophets; and above all in the Word made flesh, Jesus, your Son. For in these last days you sent him to be incarnate from the Virgin Mary, to be the Savior and Redeemer of the world. In him, you have delivered us from evil, and made us worthy to stand before you. In him, you have brought us out of error into truth, out of sin into righteousness, out of death into life.

As the words about the bread are spoken, the Celebrant holds the bread or places a hand on it; and at the words about the cup, the Celebrant holds the cup or places a hand on it and on any other container holding wine that will be consecrated.

On the night before he died for us, our Lord Jesus Christ took bread; and when he had given thanks to you, he broke it, and gave it to his disciples, and said, "Take, eat: This is my Body, which is given for you. Do this for the remembrance of me."

After supper he took the cup of wine; and when he had given thanks, he gave it to them, and said, "Drink this, all of you: This is my Blood of the new Covenant, which is shed for you and for many for the forgiveness of sins. Whenever you drink it, do this for the remembrance of me."

Therefore, according to his command, O Father,

Celebrant and People
We remember his death,
We proclaim his resurrection,
We await his coming in glory;

The Celebrant continues
And we offer our sacrifice of praise and thanksgiving to you, O Lord of all; presenting to you, from your creation, this bread and this wine.

We pray you, gracious God, to send your Holy Spirit upon these gifts that they may be the Sacrament of the Body of Christ and his Blood of the new Covenant. Unite us to your Son in his sacrifice, that we may be acceptable through him, being sanctified by the Holy Spirit. In the fullness of time, put all things in subjection under your Christ, and bring us to that heavenly country where, with [_____ and] all your saints, we may enter the everlasting heritage of your sons and daughters; through Jesus Christ our Lord, the firstborn of all creation, the head of the Church, and the author of our salvation.

By him, and with him, and in him, in the unity of the Holy Spirit all honor and glory is yours, Almighty Father, now and for ever. *Amen.*

Eucharistic Prayer C

Eucharistic Prayer C is different from the other eucharistic prayers, because in it the congregation responds frequently to what the celebrant is saying. This prayer of thanksgiving emphasizes our belief that God created the world and cares for it.

The Celebrant, whether bishop or priest, faces them and sings or says

The Lord be with you.
And also with you.

Lift up your hearts.
We lift them to the Lord.

Let us give thanks to the Lord our God.
It is right to give him thanks and praise.

Then, facing the Holy Table, the Celebrant proceeds

God of all power, Ruler of the Universe, you are worthy of glory and praise.
Glory to you for ever and ever.

At your command all things came to be: the vast expanse of interstellar space, galaxies, suns, the planets in their courses, and this fragile earth, our island home.
By your will they were created and have their being.

From the primal elements you brought forth the human race, and blessed us with memory, reason, and skill. You made us the rulers of creation. But we turned against you, and betrayed your trust; and we turned against one another.
Have mercy, Lord, for we are sinners in your sight.

Again and again, you called us to return. Through prophets and sages you revealed your righteous Law. And in the fullness of time you sent your only Son, born of a woman, to fulfill your Law, to open for us the way of freedom and peace.
By his blood, he reconciled us.
By his wounds, we are healed.

And therefore we praise you, joining with the heavenly chorus, with prophets, apostles, and martyrs, and with all those in every generation who have looked to you in hope, to proclaim with them your glory, in their unending hymn:

Celebrant and People
Holy, holy, holy Lord,
    God of power and might,
heaven and earth are full of your glory.
    Hosanna in the highest.
Blessed is he who comes in the name
    of the Lord.
    Hosanna in the highest.

The Celebrant continues
And so, Father, we who have been redeemed by him, and made a new people by water and the Spirit, now bring before you these gifts. Sanctify them by your Holy Spirit to be the Body and Blood of Jesus Christ our Lord.

As the words about the bread are spoken, the Celebrant holds the bread or places a hand on it; and at the words about the cup, the Celebrant holds the cup or places a hand on it and on any other container holding wine that will be consecrated.

On the night he was betrayed he took bread, said the blessing, broke the bread, and gave it to his friends, and said, "Take, eat: This is my Body, which is given for you. Do this for the remembrance of me."

After supper, he took the cup of wine, gave thanks, and said, "Drink this, all of you: This is my Blood of the new Covenant, which is shed for you and for many for the forgiveness of sins. Whenever you drink it, do this for the remembrance of me."

Remembering now his work of redemption, and offering to you this sacrifice of thanksgiving,
We celebrate his death and resurrection, as we await the day of his coming.

Lord God of our Fathers; God of Abraham, Isaac, and Jacob; God and Father of our Lord Jesus Christ: Open our eyes to see your hand at work in the world about us. Deliver us from the presumption of coming to this Table for solace only, and not for strength; for pardon only, and not for renewal. Let the grace of this Holy Communion make us one body, one spirit in Christ, that we may worthily serve the world in his name.

Risen Lord, be known to us in the breaking of the Bread.

Accept these prayers and praises, Father, through Jesus Christ our great High Priest, to whom, with you and the Holy Spirit, your Church gives honor, glory, and worship, from generation to generation. *Amen.*

Eucharistic Prayer D

Eucharistic Prayer D, based on a very old prayer, was written about 1500 years ago by Saint Basil, a Christian hero who lived where Turkey is today. Since this prayer is used by other Christians besides Episcopalians, it has special meaning for the unity of all Christians.

The people remain standing. The Celebrant, whether bishop or priest, faces them and sings or says

	The Lord be with you.
People	And also with you.
Celebrant	Lift up your hearts.
People	We lift them to the Lord.
Celebrant	Let us give thanks to the Lord our God.
People	It is right to give him thanks and praise.

Then, facing the Holy Table, the Celebrant proceeds

It is truly right to glorify you, Father, and to give you thanks; for you alone are God, living and true, dwelling in light inaccessible from before time and for ever.

Fountain of life and source of all goodness, you made all things and fill them with your blessing; you created them to rejoice in the splendor of your radiance.

Countless throngs of angels stand before you to serve you night and day; and, beholding the glory of your presence, they offer you unceasing praise. Joining with them, and giving voice to every creature under heaven, we acclaim you, and glorify your Name, as we sing (say),

Celebrant and People

Holy, holy, holy Lord,
    God of power and might,
heaven and earth are full of your glory.
    Hosanna in the highest.
Blessed is he who comes in the name
    of the Lord.
    Hosanna in the highest.

The people stand or kneel.

Then the Celebrant continues

We acclaim you, holy Lord, glorious in power.
Your mighty works reveal your wisdom and love.

You formed us in your own image, giving the whole world into our care, so that, in obedience to you, our Creator, we might rule and serve all your creatures. When our disobedience took us far from you, you did not abandon us to the power of death. In your mercy you came to our help, so that in seeking you we might find you. Again and again you called us into covenant with you, and through the prophets you taught us to hope for salvation.

Father, you loved the world so much that in the fullness of time you sent your only Son to be our Savior. Incarnate by the Holy Spirit, born of the Virgin Mary, he lived as one of us, yet without sin. To the poor he proclaimed the good news of salvation; to prisoners, freedom; to the sorrowful, joy. To fulfill your purpose he gave himself up to death; and, rising from the grave, destroyed death, and made the whole creation new.

And, that we might live no longer for ourselves, but for him who died and rose for us, he sent the Holy Spirit, his own first gift for those who believe, to complete his work in the world, and to bring to fulfillment the sanctification of all.

As the words about the bread are spoken, the Celebrant holds the bread or places a hand on it; and at the words about the cup, the Celebrant holds the cup or places a hand on it and on any other container holding wine that will be consecrated.

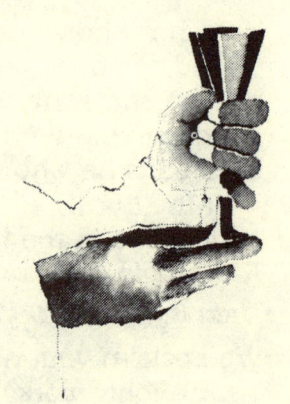

When the hour had come for him to be glorified by you, his heavenly Father, having loved his own who were in the world, he loved them to the end; at supper with them he took bread, and when he had given thanks to you, he broke it, and gave it to his disciples, and said, "Take, eat: This is my Body, which is given for you. Do this for the remembrance of me."

After supper he took the cup of wine; and when he had given thanks, he gave it to them, and said, "Drink this, all of you: This is my Blood of the new Covenant, which is shed for you and for many for the forgiveness of sins. Whenever you drink it, do this for the remembrance of me."

Father, we now celebrate this memorial of our redemption. Recalling Christ's death and his descent among the dead, proclaiming his resurrection and ascension to your right hand, awaiting his coming in glory; and offering to you, from the gifts you have given us, this bread and this cup, we praise you and we bless you.

Celebrant and People

We praise you, we bless you,
we give thanks to you,
and we pray to you, Lord Our God.

The Celebrant continues

Lord, we pray that in your goodness and mercy your Holy Spirit may descend upon us, and upon these gifts, sanctifying them and showing them to be holy gifts for your holy people, the bread of life and the cup of salvation, the Body and Blood of your Son Jesus Christ.

Grant that all who share this bread and cup may become one body and one spirit, a living sacrifice in Christ, to the praise of your Name.

Remember, Lord, your one holy catholic and apostolic Church, redeemed by the blood of your Christ. Reveal its unity, guard its faith, and preserve it in peace.

[Remember (*NN.* and) all who minister in your Church.]

[Remember all your people, and those who seek your truth.]

[Remember _____ .]

[Remember all who have died in the peace of Christ, and those whose faith is known to you alone; bring them into the place of eternal joy and light.]

And grant that we may find our inheritance with [the Blessed Virgin Mary, with patriarchs, prophets, apostles, and martyrs, (with _____) and] all the saints who have found favor with you in ages past. We praise you in union with them and give you glory through your Son Jesus Christ our Lord.

Through Christ, and with Christ, and in Christ, all honor and glory are yours, Almighty God and Father, in the unity of the Holy Spirit, for ever and ever. *Amen.*

The Lord's Prayer

All four forms of the Eucharistic Prayer end with the prayer that Jesus taught us, the Lord's Prayer. Like the Apostles' Creed, this prayer gives us the big picture of the story of Jesus. The Lord's Prayer tells us what Jesus did and what that means for our lives today. Christians have been saying this prayer at the end of the Eucharistic Prayer for 1600 years.

The Lord's Prayer was first written in Greek. We can say it in two different ways. The first one is the older version that most adults learned when they were children. It was translated over 400 years ago. The second version is a modern translation done by a group of English-speaking Christians from several countries. Which one do you prefer?

The Celebrant continues
And now, as our Savior
Christ has taught us,
we are bold to say,

Or the following
As our Savior Christ
has taught us,
we now pray,

People and Celebrant
Our Father, who art in heaven,
   hallowed be thy Name,
   thy kingdom come,
   thy will be done,
     on earth as it is in heaven.
Give us this day our daily bread.
And forgive us our trespasses,
   as we forgive those
     who trespass against us.
And lead us not into temptation,
   but deliver us from evil.
For thine is the kingdom,
   and the power, and the glory,
   for ever and ever. Amen.

Or the following
Our Father in heaven,
   hallowed be your Name,
   your kingdom come,
   your will be done,
     on earth as in heaven.
Give us today our daily bread.

Forgive us our sins
  as we forgive those
    who sin against us.
Save us from the time of trial,
  and deliver us from evil.
For the kingdom, the power,
  and the glory are yours,
    now and for ever. Amen.

The Breaking of the Bread

Our worship tells a story—in words and in actions. The Eucharist is a play about what Jesus did the night before he died on the cross. When you read the story in the New Testament, you will find that Jesus took the bread and wine, said a prayer over it, broke the bread, and then gave the bread and the wine to his apostles to eat and drink. These are the four things he did. We have already done two of these in the first two parts of Holy Communion. In the Offertory *we took the bread and wine.* In the Great Thanksgiving *we said a prayer over it.* Now we come to the third part, the *breaking of the bread.* Watch while the priest breaks the bread. Listen. The church is especially quiet.

Then may be sung or said

[Alleluia.] Christ our Passover is sacrificed for us; *Therefore let us keep the feast.* [*Alleluia.*]

In Lent, Alleluia is left out, and may be left out at other times except during Easter Season.

Some other suitable anthem may be used instead of the one above, or in addition to it.

---

68   Praying with the Family of God

The Eating and Drinking

Now we come to the fourth part of Holy Communion, *the eating and drinking of the bread and wine.* We go up to the altar for the bread and wine, which to us are the heavenly Body and Blood of Jesus. We can enjoy the taste of the food, and we can give thanks for the new life and love that we experience in being with one another and with God. Remember how good Tim thought the turkey and dressing tasted and how happy Tim was that they all could be together, giving thanks for being alive and sharing in one another's love? Holy Communion is something like that.

Facing the people, the Celebrant says

The Gifts of God for the People of God.

and may add

Take them in remembrance that
Christ died for you, and feed on him
in your hearts by faith, with
thanksgiving.

The ministers receive the Sacrament in both kinds, and then immediately deliver it to the people.

The Bread and the Cup are given to the communicants with these words

The Body (Blood) of our Lord Jesus Christ keep you in everlasting life. [*Amen.*]

or with these words

The Body of Christ, the bread of heaven. [*Amen.*]
The Blood of Christ, the cup of salvation. [*Amen.*]

During the ministration of Communion, hymns, psalms, or anthems may be sung.

The Ending

Holy Communion is now over. Before we leave the church, we pause to thank God for the gift of new life through Jesus. The celebrant will choose one of these two prayers of thanksgiving. After this prayer the priest sometimes gives us a blessing. Then we are sent out of the church with a call to serve God in everything we do. As we leave, we know that God loves us so much that he sent Jesus to die and to rise so that we could have good lives.

After Communion, the Celebrant says
Let us pray.

Celebrant and People

Eternal God, heavenly Father,
you have graciously accepted us
   as living members
of your Son our Savior Jesus Christ,
and you have fed us with spiritual food
in the Sacrament of his Body and Blood.
Send us now into the world in peace,
and grant us strength and courage
to love and serve you
with gladness and singleness of heart;
through Christ our Lord. Amen.

or the following

Almighty and everliving God,
we thank you for feeding us
   with the spiritual food
of the most precious Body and Blood
of your Son our Savior Jesus Christ;

and for assuring us in these holy mysteries
that we are living members
   of the Body of your Son,
and heirs of your eternal kingdom.
And now, Father, send us out
to do the work you have given us to do,
to love and serve you
as faithful witnesses of Christ our Lord.
To him, to you, and to the Holy Spirit,
be honor and glory,
   now and for ever. Amen.

The Bishop when present, or the Priest, may bless the people.

The Deacon, or the Celebrant, dismisses them with these words

            Let us go forth in the name of Christ.
People   Thanks be to God.

or this

Deacon   Go in peace to love and serve the Lord.

People   Thanks be to God.

or this

Deacon   Let us go forth into the world,
            rejoicing in the power of the Spirit.
People   Thanks be to God.

or this

Deacon   Let us bless the Lord.
People   Thanks be to God.

From the Easter Vigil through the Day of Pentecost the words "Alleluia, alleluia" may be added to any of the dismissals.

The People respond
            Thanks be to God. Alleluia, alleluia.

Special Days

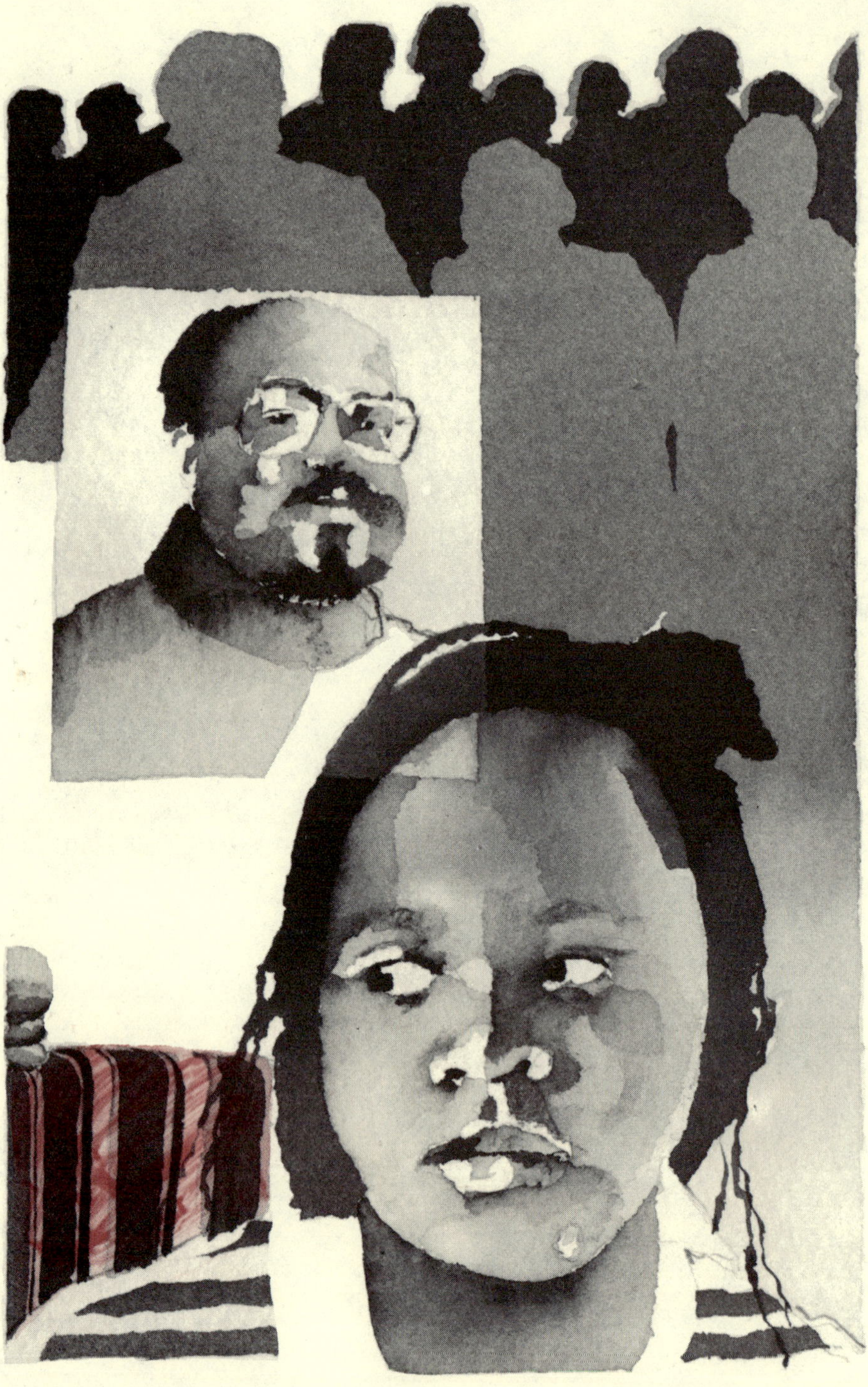

Ruth lived in a tall apartment building with her mother and her grandmother. Every morning she walked to the corner where she waited for the school bus with lots of other black kids from the same apartment building. The bus took them to a school on the other side of town. Most of the kids at the school were white.

Ruth thought school was okay, but a lot of the time she felt confused. Almost all the books were about white kids, and sometimes she had trouble understanding the things they talked about in class. On the playground she usually played by herself. She felt different from the other kids.

One time she felt that way was during spelling. The teacher wrote "ancestor" on the board. He spelled it out loud, slowly, and then he asked if anybody knew what an ancestor was. David Fort raised his hand. He always knew everything. "My grandfather was an ancestor," he started. Then he went on and on, telling the whole class how his grandfather was a hero in the war and how he won a lot of medals for being brave and getting hurt. Big deal. Ruth stared out the window.

That night Ruth felt pretty bad. She thought about David Fort. She thought about how she didn't know her own grandfather. She didn't even know her father. She sank down into the big living room chair and looked at the wall. Her grandmother came in from the kitchen. She knew that look.

"Child, what're you looking so sad for?" she asked. So Ruth told her about David Fort and his ancestor.

Her grandmother smiled as she smoothed out the collar on Ruth's dress. "Child," she began, "did you know your grandfather marched with Dr. Martin Luther King?"

"Who's Dr. King?" Ruth asked without looking up. Her grandmother settled down in the chair next to Ruth and told Ruth a story. She explained that Dr. King was a Christian minister who marched down the streets and highways of Alabama, and then many other states, to let white people know how much black people suffered and how things ought to change. Many people listened to Dr. King. He made a lot of changes for black people before he was killed on April 4, 1968.

"Your grandfather," Ruth's grandma said, "was in jail with Dr. King in Birmingham, Alabama. He was with him on the march to Selma, and he was with him the night before he was murdered in Memphis, Tennessee." She lowered her voice to a whisper. "Your grandfather marched for our freedom."

Ruth sat in that chair for a long time. She thought about what her grandma had told her, and the longer she thought, the better she felt. Then she remembered David, and she grinned. It was okay to be different from him, she decided. That didn't make her less important. She had a story about an ancestor, just like David did. Her grandfather was a hero too.

Ruth found out that when she knew her family story, she could better understand who she was. She didn't feel so lonely anymore, and being different wasn't so hard. Christians have a family story just like Ruth did.

One way to hear the family story is to have special days to remember important parts of the story. Your birthday, your parents' wedding anniversary, the Fourth of July—these are special days that tell a story. The Church has special days too, to remember what Jesus did. Ruth's grandfather was with Dr. King at Birmingham, Selma, and Memphis; Jesus went into Jerusalem, he washed the feet of his disciples and had the Last Supper with them, he died on the Cross and was raised from the dead—all in one week! We call this special week Holy Week and Easter.

Your prayer book shows ways to celebrate these and other special events and to remember the story of Jesus. When we celebrate these special days, we are remembering our Christian story. We are finding out who we are.

What Happens on Special Days

Ash Wednesday
    The Collect of the Day
    The Invitation
    Thy Symbol of the Ashes
    The Psalm
    The Litany of Penitence
    The Absolution

The Sunday of the Passion: Palm Sunday
    The Liturgy of the Palms
    The Prayer
    The Blessing
    The Procession

Maundy Thursday
    The Collect of the Day
    The Ceremony of the Washing of Feet
    The Eucharist

Good Friday
    The Beginning
    The Solemn Collects
    The Veneration of the Cross
    The Anthems
    The Holy Communion
    The Prayer

The Great Vigil of Easter
    Lighting the Paschal Candle
    The Liturgy of the Word
    Baptism and Renewal of Baptismal Vows
    At the Eucharist

Ash Wednesday

Ash Wednesday is different from the other special days in this prayer book because it does not celebrate an event in the life of Jesus. Ash Wednesday begins the season of Lent.

Lent lasts for forty days, not counting the Sundays, and ends with Easter. Lent is the church season of sadness and repentance that prepares us for the joy and new life of Easter. The forty days of Lent come from the forty days that Jesus fasted in the desert. Like Jesus, we use these forty days as a preparation time.

The custom of putting ashes on our foreheads began long ago when people used the ashes as a way to express sadness. In the Old Testament, Job thinks about his sins and says "I repent in dust and ashes." Job is saying that ashes show repentance. This practice of using ashes to make a cross on the forehead is over 1100 years old. When we have the priest make the sign of the cross in ashes on our foreheads, we are saying "I am sorry for my sins." Some churches still practice this custom.

The Collect of the Day

On Ash Wednesday we use the service of the Holy Eucharist. It begins with this special collect.

> *The Celebrant begins*
> Let us pray.
> Almighty and everlasting God, you hate nothing you have made and forgive the sins of all who are penitent: Create and make in us new and contrite

Special Days

hearts, that we, worthily lamenting our sins and acknowledging our wretchedness, may obtain of you, the God of all mercy, perfect remission and forgiveness; through Jesus Christ our Lord, who lives and reigns with you and the Holy Spirit, one God, for ever and ever. *Amen.*

The Invitation

After the sermon the priest invites us to begin the season of Lent by praying, fasting, giving up something we like, reading and meditating on the Word of God. The priest's invitation also explains how the season of Lent was used by the early Christians. For us, this season is a time to look at ourselves, to measure ourselves against what we would like to be. The feelings of this season are sadness—for not being all we could be—and determination—as we try to be strong and firm with ourselves so that we can become the kind of people we want to be. These feelings help prepare us for the celebration that comes with Easter.

After the Sermon, everyone stands, and the Celebrant or Minister appointed invites the people to the observance of a holy Lent, saying

Dear People of God: The first Christians observed with great devotion the days of our Lord's passion and resurrection, and it became the custom of the Church to prepare for them by a season of penitence and fasting. This season of Lent provided a time in which converts to the faith were prepared for Holy Baptism. It was also a time when those who, because of notorious sins, had been separated from the body of the faithful were reconciled by penitence and forgiveness, and restored to the fellowship of the Church. Thereby, the whole congregation was put in mind of the message of pardon and absolution set forth in the Gospel of our Savior, and of the need which all Christians continually have to renew their repentance and faith.

I invite you, therefore, in the name of the Church, to the observance of a holy Lent, by self-examination and repentance; by prayer, fasting, and self-denial; and by reading and meditating on God's holy Word. And, to make a right beginning of repentance, and as a mark of our mortal nature, let us now kneel before the Lord, our maker and redeemer.

Everyone kneels in silence.

The Symbol of the Ashes

If it is the custom in your church and if you wish, you may go to the front and receive the sign of the cross in ashes. As you kneel or stand and have the sign of the cross put on your forehead, the priest will say words which remind us that we are all like Adam and Eve in the Old Testament: We have come from the earth, and we shall return to the earth.

If ashes are to be used, the Celebrant says the following prayer

Almighty God, you have created us out of the dust of the earth: Grant that these ashes may be to us a sign of our mortality and penitence, that we may remember that it is only by your gracious gift that we are given everlasting life; through Jesus Christ our Savior. *Amen.*

The ashes are marked on people's foreheads with the following words

Remember that you are dust, and to dust you shall return.

The Psalm

The psalms are Old Testament poems. As people read or sang the psalms, they often played a stringed instrument similar to a guitar. Psalm 51 is one of the great Jewish prayers for forgiveness. Listen to the sadness. Imagine how the poet felt.

The following is sung or said. (An asterisk divides each verse into two parts for reading or chanting. In reading, pause at the asterisk.)

Psalm 51   *Miserere mei, Deus*

Have mercy on me, O God, according
 to your loving-kindness;*
  in your great compassion blot out my
   offenses.
Wash me through and through
 from my wickedness*
  and cleanse me from my sin.
For I know my transgressions,*
  and my sin is ever before me.
Against you only have I sinned*
  and done what is evil in your sight.
And so you are justified when you speak*
  and upright in your judgment.
Indeed, I have been wicked from my birth,*
  a sinner from my mother's womb.
For behold, you look for truth
 deep within me,*
  and will make me understand
   wisdom secretly.

Purge me from my sin, and I shall be pure;*
 wash me, and I shall be clean indeed.
Make me hear of joy and gladness,*
 that the body you have broken
  may rejoice.
Hide your face from my sins*
 and blot out all my iniquities.
Create in me a clean heart, O God,*
 and renew a right spirit within me.
Cast me not away from your presence*
 and take not your holy Spirit from me.
Give me the joy of your saving help again*
 and sustain me with your bountiful
  Spirit.
I shall teach your ways to the wicked,*
 and sinners shall return to you.
Deliver me from death, O God,*
 and my tongue shall sing
  of your righteousness,
 O God of my salvation.
Open my lips, O Lord,*
 and my mouth shall proclaim your praise.
Had you desired it, I would have
  offered sacrifice;*
 but you take no delight
  in burnt-offerings.
The sacrifice of God is a troubled spirit;*
 a broken and contrite heart, O God,
  you will not despise.

The Litany of Penitence

A litany is a form of prayer that we use often during Lent. The word *litany* means *prayer*. It also means a kind of prayer in which the leader makes a request to God, and the people respond, back and forth. Many of the responses are the same. The simple back-and-forth rhythm of the litany reminds us of the sorrow we feel during Lent. This litany is a confession of our sins.

The Celebrant and People together, all kneeling

Most holy and merciful Father:
We confess to you and to one another,
and to the whole communion of saints
in heaven and on earth,
that we have sinned by our own fault
in thought, word, and deed;
by what we have done, and by what
   we have left undone.

The Celebrant continues

We have not loved you with our whole heart, and mind, and strength. We have not loved our neighbors as ourselves. We have not forgiven others, as we have been forgiven.
Have mercy on us, Lord.

We have been deaf to your call to serve, as Christ served us. We have not been true to the mind of Christ. We have grieved your Holy Spirit.
Have mercy on us, Lord.

We confess to you, Lord, all our past unfaithfulness: the pride, hypocrisy, and impatience of our lives,
We confess to you, Lord.

Our self-indulgent appetites and ways, and our exploitation of other people,
We confess to you, Lord.

Our anger at our own frustration, and our envy of those more fortunate than ourselves,
We confess to you, Lord.

Our intemperate love of worldly goods and comforts, and our dishonesty in daily life and work,
We confess to you, Lord.

Our negligence in prayer and worship, and our failure to commend the faith that is in us,
We confess to you, Lord.

Accept our repentance, Lord, for the wrongs we have done: for our blindness to human need and suffering, and our indifference to injustice and cruelty,
Accept our repentance, Lord.

For all false judgments, for uncharitable thoughts toward our neighbors, and for our prejudice and contempt toward those who differ from us,
Accept our repentance, Lord.

For our waste and pollution of your creation, and our lack of concern for those who come after us,
Accept our repentance, Lord.

Restore us, good Lord, and let your anger depart from us;
Favorably hear us, for your mercy is great.

Accomplish in us the work of your salvation,
That we may show forth your glory in the world.

By the cross and passion of your Son our Lord,
Bring us with all your saints to the joy of his resurrection.

The Absolution

During the litany we confessed our sins. Now, in the absolution, we are forgiven. *Absolution* means *setting someone free.* In this case, we are set free from our sins. Jesus gave this power of forgiveness to the Church so that his people could be free to love God more happily and more completely. The bishop or the priest who says the absolution represents the Church. If you think of your sins as acts that separate you from God and from others in God's family, then you can imagine how the absolution can set you free.

The Bishop, if present, or the Priest, stands and faces the people, saying

Almighty God, the Father of our Lord Jesus Christ, who desires not the death of sinners, but rather that they may turn from their wickedness and live, has given power and commandment to his ministers to declare and pronounce to his people, being penitent, the absolution and remission of their sins. He pardons and absolves all those who truly repent, and with sincere hearts believe his holy Gospel.

Therefore we beseech him to grant us true repentance and his Holy Spirit, that those things may please him which we do on this day, and that the rest of our life hereafter may be pure and holy, so that at the last we may come to his eternal joy; through Jesus Christ our Lord. *Amen.*

The Peace is then exchanged.

The Sunday of the Passion: Palm Sunday

The last week of Lent is Holy Week. This week and the week of Easter that follows are the most important days of the Christian year. Palm Sunday is the first day of Holy Week, exactly seven days before Easter. The older name for this day is the Sunday of Passion. On this day we read from one of the four Gospels about the death of Jesus on the Cross, and so we call this Sunday the Sunday of the Passion, or suffering, of Jesus. Although it is a day of joyful celebration, it is also the beginning of the week of the crucifixion.

On Palm Sunday we celebrate Jesus' ride through the streets of Jerusalem. People lined the streets and waved palm branches as he rode by them on a donkey. Many people hailed him as the Messiah who had been described by an Old Testament prophet.

Rejoice, rejoice, people of Zion!
    Shout for joy, you people of Jerusalem!
    Look, your king is coming to you!
He comes triumphant and victorious,
    but humble and riding on a donkey—
    on a colt, the foal of a donkey.
                      (Zechariah 9:9-10)

The Liturgy of the Palms

Jesus' happy ride through the streets of Jerusalem happened during a religious celebration, when people were parading around the city walls singing and carrying palm branches. They sang the words "Blessed is the king who comes in the name of the Lord." We celebrate Palm Sunday by repeating the palm-carrying and singing that happened in Jerusalem one week before Jesus died.

The following or some other suitable anthem is sung or said as the people stand.

Blessed is the King who comes in the name of the Lord:

Peace in heaven and glory in the highest.

Special Days

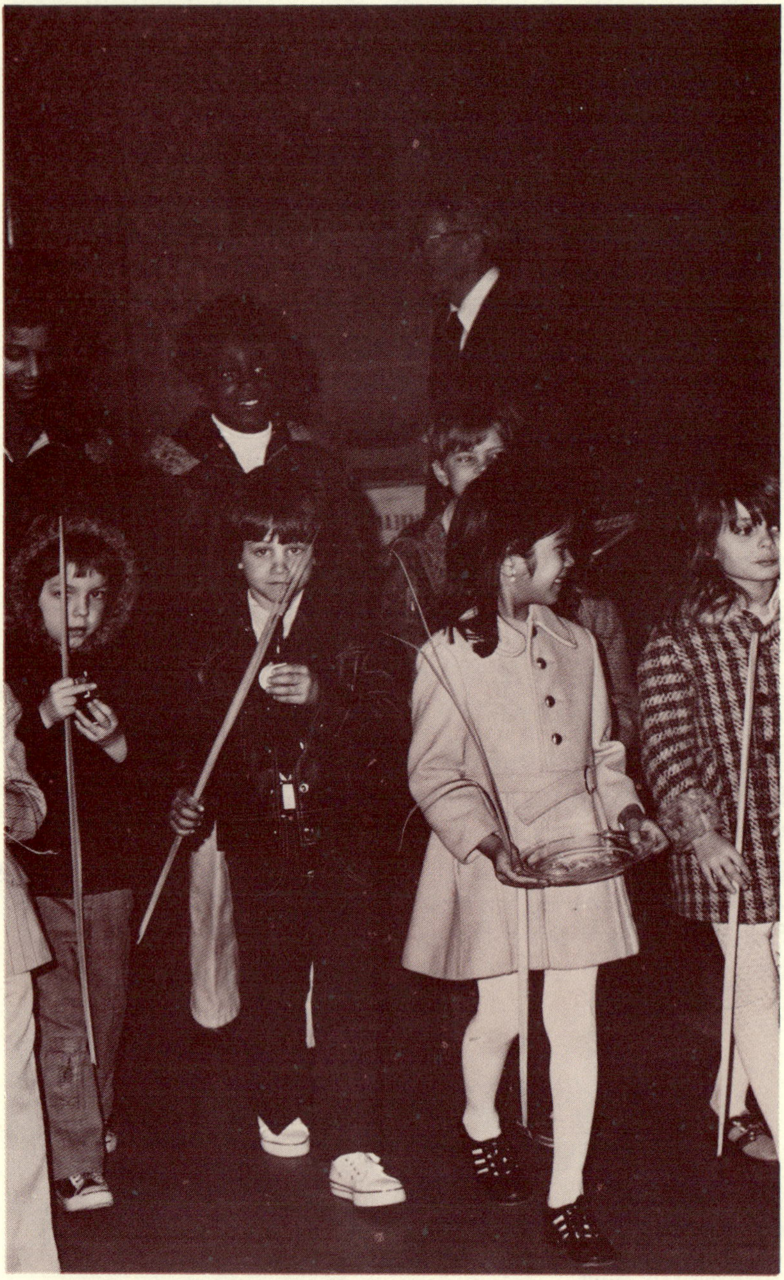

The Prayer

This prayer for Palm Sunday tells us what Holy Week and Easter are all about. We are preparing ourselves for this important week by remembering the "mighty acts" of Jesus—the things he did to set us free. We are stronger when we remember what Jesus did for us, just as Ruth was stronger and surer of herself after hearing the story of her grandfather.

Celebrant   Let us pray.

Assist us mercifully with your help, O Lord God of our salvation, that we may enter with joy upon the contemplation of those mighty acts, whereby you have given us life and immortality; through Jesus Christ our Lord. *Amen.*

Here a Deacon or other person appointed reads from the Bible about Jesus' acting out the words of Zechariah.

The Blessing

The priest will now bless the palms or tree branches. A palm stands for victory—the victory of Jesus as we are united with God. The palms take on this special meaning as the priest blesses them.

The Celebrant says
	The Lord be with you.
People	And also with you.
Celebrant	Let us give thanks to the Lord our God.
People	It is right to give him thanks and praise.

Special Days

It is right to praise you, Almighty God, for the acts of love by which you have redeemed us through your Son Jesus Christ our Lord. On this day he entered the holy city of Jerusalem in triumph, and was proclaimed as King of kings by those who spread their garments and branches of palm along his way. Let these branches be for us signs of his victory, and grant that we who bear them in his name may ever hail him as our King, and follow him in the way that leads to eternal life; who lives and reigns in glory with you and the Holy Spirit, now and for ever. *Amen.*

The following or some other suitable anthem may then be sung or said

Blessed is he who comes in the name of the Lord. *Hosanna in the highest.*

The Procession

Just as the people paraded in Jerusalem so long ago, we will now parade inside or around our church. We thank God for sending Jesus to free us from loneliness and fear.

Deacon Let us go forth in peace;
People In the name of Christ. Amen.

During the procession, all hold branches in their hands, and appropriate hymns, psalms, or anthems are sung, such as the hymn "All glory, laud, and honor" and Psalm 118:19-29.

At a suitable place, the procession may stop while the following or some other appropriate Collect is said

Almighty God, whose most dear Son went not up to joy but first he suffered pain, and entered not

into glory before he was crucified: Mercifully grant
that we, walking in the way of the cross, may find
it none other than the way of life and peace;
through Jesus Christ our Lord. *Amen.*

The worship now continues with the Holy Eucharist. Your church may divide the Bible reading into parts so that you and the other parishioners will be the people asking Pontius Pilate to crucify Jesus. This reading will help you remember that the same people who hailed Jesus as their king on Palm Sunday were shouting for his crucifixion only a few days later. Underneath our celebration of the Palm Sunday parade there is also our sadness when we remember the lack of faith that brought Jesus' death.

Maundy Thursday

Maundy Thursday is the Thursday of Holy Week, the day before Jesus died. The word *maundy* comes from a word meaning *commandment.* On this day Jesus gave us a new commandment.

This is also the day that Jesus shared his last supper with the apostles. We call this meal "the Holy Eucharist." As we eat the bread and drink the wine together at the Eucharist, Jesus says we eat his Body and drink his Blood. The Eucharist keeps us aware that Jesus is with us. When we receive the Eucharist, we are acting out the death and resurrection of Jesus. Holy Communion helps us know the power of God's love as he brings us close to him.

Maundy Thursday is the day Jesus gave us the new commandment to love one another as he loves us. Jesus acted out this commandment with a surprising gesture: he washed the feet of his followers. In Jesus' time this was a job that not even a slave was asked to do. It was considered lower than washing the floor or taking out the garbage. When Jesus washed his followers' feet, he showed them how much he loved them. He loves us all this much, and he tells us to share this same love with each other.

Your priest may wash the feet of some of the people in your church in order to show the meaning of love the way Jesus did. Maybe you'll be one of the people whose feet will be washed by the priest.

The Collect of the Day

The special service for Maundy Thursday fits into the regular Holy Eucharist service, beginning with this collect.

> Almighty Father, whose dear Son, on the night before he suffered, instituted the Sacrament of his Body and Blood: Mercifully grant that we may receive it thankfully in remembrance of Jesus Christ our Lord, who in these holy mysteries gives us a pledge of eternal life; and who now lives and reigns with you and the Holy Spirit, one God, for ever and ever. *Amen.*
>
> *The Psalm and lessons are then read.*

The Ceremony of the Washing of Feet

If your priest is going to wash people's feet, try to get close enough to watch.

When it occurs, the ceremony of the washing of feet appropriately follows the Gospel and homily.

During the ceremony, the following or other suitable anthems may be sung or said

The Lord Jesus, after he had supped with his disciples and had washed their feet, said to them, "Do you know what I, your Lord and Master, have done to you? I have given you an example, that you should do as I have done."

Peace is my last gift to you, my own peace I now leave with you; peace which the world cannot give, I give to you.

I give you a new commandment: Love one another as I have loved you.

Peace is my last gift to you, my own peace I now leave with you; peace which the world cannot give, I give to you.

By this shall the world know that you are my disciples: That you have love for one another.

The service continues with the Prayers of the People.

The Eucharist

As you begin Holy Communion, remember that Maundy Thursday celebrates the very first eucharistic meal.

Good Friday

This is a sad day. Today's worship service doesn't include the Eucharist because we think of the Eucharist as a happy event. Our worship today follows the Way of the Cross; that is, we accompany Jesus as he makes his journey to his death. Then why do we call today *Good Friday*? What's good about such a sad day?

Good Friday leads to Easter, to the resurrection of Jesus and new life for all of us. We know that Jesus' death on the Cross was not the end but the beginning. Even though we remember his pain and suffering on this day, we also remember the good news that his death has saved us. And so, even though it is sad, this is a *Good* Friday.

The Beginning

The Bible reading, called the Passion Gospel, tells us about what happened to Jesus on this day. This story of his suffering and death is sometimes divided into parts for people to read. This is also the way the Gospel can be read on Palm Sunday. You and the other parishioners will take the part of the crowd who wanted Jesus crucified.

On this day the ministers enter in silence.

All then kneel for silent prayer, after which the Celebrant stands and begins the liturgy with the Collect of the Day.

Immediately before the Collect, the Celebrant may say
    Blessed be our God,
People For ever and ever. Amen.

Let us pray.

Almighty God, we pray you graciously to behold this your family, for whom our Lord Jesus Christ was willing to be betrayed, and given into the hands of sinners, and to suffer death upon the cross; who now lives and reigns with you and the Holy Spirit, one God, for ever and ever. *Amen.*

The Passion Gospel is announced with these words
The Passion of our Lord Jesus Christ according to John.

The regular responses before and after the Gospel are not spoken.

The Passion Gospel may be read or chanted by lay persons. Specific roles may be assigned to different persons, and the congregation may take the part of the crowd.

The congregation may be seated for the first part of the Passion. At the verse which mentions the arrival at Golgotha (John 19:17) all stand.

The Sermon follows. A hymn may then be sung.

The Solemn Collects

The Solemn Collects, or prayers, are like the Prayers of the People in the Eucharist. *Solemn* comes from two Greek words meaning *all year.* This name tells us that everything we have said and done *all year* comes together now, as we pray for God's help and love.

A bidding prayer, which is the form of the Solemn Collects on Good Friday, is a prayer that begins "Let us pray for" and continues with some specific request. It asks or "bids" for something. This form of bidding prayer on Good Friday has been the custom in the Western Church for over 1000 years.

Everyone stands as the Deacon, or other person appointed, says to the people

Dear People of God: Our heavenly Father sent his Son into the world, not to condemn the world, but that the world through him might be saved; that all who believe in him might be delivered from the power of sin and death, and become heirs with him of everlasting life.

We pray, therefore, for people everywhere according to their needs.

The bidding may be read by a Deacon or other selected person. The Celebrant says the Collects.

Let us pray for the holy Catholic Church of Christ throughout the world;
    For its unity in witness and service
    For all bishops and other ministers
        and the people whom they serve
    For *N.*, our Bishop, and all the
        people of this diocese
    For all Christians in this community
    For those about to be baptized
        (particularly _____)
That God will confirm his Church in faith, increase it in love, and preserve it in peace.

Silence

Almighty and everlasting God, by whose Spirit the whole body of your faithful people is governed and sanctified: Receive our supplications and prayers which we offer before you for all members of your holy Church, that in their vocation and ministry they may truly and devoutly serve you; through our Lord and Savior Jesus Christ. *Amen.*

Let us pray for all nations and peoples of the earth, and for those in authority among them;
    For *N.*, the President of the
        United States
    For the Congress and the Supreme Court
    For the Members and Representatives
        of the United Nations
    For all who serve the common good
That by God's help they may seek justice and truth, and live in peace and concord.

Silence

Almighty God, kindle, we pray, in every heart the true love of peace, and guide with your wisdom

those who take counsel for the nations of the earth;
that in tranquillity your dominion may increase,
until the earth is filled with the knowledge of your
love; through Jesus Christ our Lord. *Amen.*

Let us pray for all who suffer and are afflicted in
body or in mind;
> For the hungry and the homeless,
>> the destitute and the oppressed
>
> For the sick, the wounded,
>> and the crippled
>
> For those in loneliness, fear,
>> and anguish
>
> For those who face temptation,
>> doubt, and despair
>
> For the sorrowful and bereaved
>
> For prisoners and captives,
>> and those in mortal danger

That God in his mercy will comfort and relieve
them, and grant them the knowledge of his love,
and stir up in us the will and patience to minister
to their needs.

Silence

Gracious God, the comfort of all who sorrow, the
strength of all who suffer: Let the cry of those in
misery and need come to you, that they may find
your mercy present with them in all their
afflictions; and give us, we pray, the strength to
serve them for the sake of him who suffered for
us, your Son Jesus Christ our Lord. *Amen.*

Let us pray for all who have not received the
Gospel of Christ;
> For those who have never heard the
>> word of salvation
>
> For those who have lost their faith

> For those hardened by sin
>   or indifference
> For the contemptuous and the scornful
> For those who are enemies of the cross
>   of Christ and persecutors
>   of his disciples
> For those who in the name of Christ
>   have persecuted others
> That God will open their hearts to the truth, and lead them to faith and obedience.

Silence

Merciful God, creator of all the peoples of the earth and lover of souls: Have compassion on all who do not know you as you are revealed in your Son Jesus Christ; let your Gospel be preached with grace and power to those who have not heard it; turn the hearts of those who resist it; and bring home to your fold those who have gone astray; that there may be one flock under one shepherd, Jesus Christ our Lord. *Amen.*

Let us commit ourselves to our God, and pray for the grace of a holy life, that, with all who have departed this world and have died in the peace of Christ, and those whose faith is known to God alone, we may be accounted worthy to enter into the fullness of the joy of our Lord, and receive the crown of life in the day of resurrection.

Silence

This last prayer in the Solemn Collects reminds us of something very important that Christians believe. Although, like Jesus, people and things grow old and die, God has a plan for everything. Like Jesus, everything will be raised up and made new.

O God of unchangeable power and eternal light: Look favorably on your whole Church, that wonderful and sacred mystery; by the effectual working of your providence, carry out in tranquillity the plan of salvation; let the whole world see and know that things which were cast down are being raised up, and things which had grown old are being made new, and that all things are being brought to their perfection by him through whom all things were made, your Son Jesus Christ our Lord; who lives and reigns with you, in the unity of the Holy Spirit, one God, for ever and ever. *Amen.*

The service may be concluded here with the singing of a hymn or anthem, the Lord's Prayer, and the final prayer on page 102.

The Veneration of the Cross

Some worship services for Good Friday continue with a reminder of the Way of the Cross. Sometimes this is called the Veneration of the Cross. When we venerate the cross we think of what Jesus did for us. By honoring the cross in our church, we can show love for Jesus and give thanks to him. Just as we keep a medal or a souvenir to remind us of something important that happened to us, the cross reminds us of Jesus' love.

What you do at the Veneration of the Cross depends on the custom of your church. In some churches you will have an opportunity to go up to the cross, to kneel, and to kiss the feet of the figure of Jesus on the cross.

In other places, particularly those that use a cross without Jesus on it, you may simply kneel and bow before the cross. In still other churches, the custom is for you to remain at your seat.

The Anthems

If these words are spoken instead of sung, the people read the parts that are in italics.

Anthem 1

We glory in your cross, O Lord,
and praise and glorify your
holy resurrection;
for by virtue of your cross
joy has come to the whole world.

May God be merciful to us
and bless us,
show us the light of his countenance,
and come to us.

Let your ways be known upon earth,
your saving health among all nations.

Let the peoples praise you, O God;
let all the peoples praise you.

We glory in your cross, O Lord,
and praise and glorify your
holy resurrection;
for by virtue of your cross
joy has come to the whole world.

Anthem 2

We adore you, O Christ, and we bless you,
because by your holy cross you have
redeemed the world.

If we have died with him,
we shall also live with him;
if we endure, we shall also
reign with him.

We adore you, O Christ, and we bless you, because by your holy cross you have redeemed the world.

Anthem 3

O Savior of the world,
who by thy cross and precious blood
   hast redeemed us:
*Save us and help us, we humbly
   beseech thee, O Lord.*

The hymn "Sing, my tongue, the glorious battle," or some other hymn praising the glory of the cross, is then sung.

The service may be concluded here with the Lord's Prayer and the final prayer.

The Holy Communion

Holy Communion is not always offered at the Good Friday service. When it is, we use the bread and wine that are already consecrated. Before taking communion, we say the Confession of Sin and the Lord's Prayer.

The Prayer

Church services usually end with words that mean *this is the end*. We may sing the words. Just as stories sometimes end with ". . . and so they lived happily ever after," these words tell us the story is finished.

But the Good Friday service is different. It doesn't end with words that mean *this is the end* because we know it is not the end. Easter is on Sunday. And Easter can't really be separated from Good Friday. They are part of one event. The service ends with the following prayer, without a blessing or a dismissal.

Lord Jesus Christ, Son of the living God, we pray you to set your passion, cross, and death between your judgment and our souls, now and in the hour of our death. Give mercy and grace to the living; pardon and rest to the dead; to your holy Church peace and concord; and to us sinners everlasting life and glory; for with the Father and Holy Spirit you live and reign, one God, now and for ever. *Amen.*

The Great Vigil of Easter

This vigil, when it occurs, is the first service of Easter Day. It is celebrated between sunset on Holy Saturday and sunrise on Easter Morning. When the Vigil is not celebrated, the lighting of the Paschal Candle may take place at a convenient time before the service on Easter Sunday.

Easter Sunday is the most important day in the church year. Every service throughout the year tells and acts out a story, and the story of this service is the most important one of all. During Holy Week we have marched with Jesus into Jerusalem, waving the branches of trees and declaring that he is the person who has come to set us free. We have also been with Jesus at his last supper when he said he would come to us whenever we remember him by eating bread and drinking wine together. We were there when he washed our feet and told us to love one another as he loves us. We were with him on Good Friday, when he died on the Cross so that his love could overcome all the hate that separates us from God.

Now, on Easter, we are with Jesus again, and now he is risen from the grave. This is a joyful and wonderful moment. We are glad together. Our lives have been saved by the great love of Jesus.

Lighting the Paschal Candle

The service begins in the dark, bringing us back to Good Friday. Then suddenly there is light—from the beautiful paschal candle. The light reminds us that Jesus is the light of the world. The word *paschal* is a Jewish word that means *passover,* the great Jewish festival that celebrates the time God freed the Hebrews from slavery in Egypt. Easter is the Christian paschal festival that celebrates when Jesus "passed over" from death to life for us. We believe God freed us from our sins at the first Easter, just as God freed the Hebrews from their Egyptian masters.

> *The celebrant may begin*
> Dear friends in Christ: On this most holy night, in which our Lord Jesus passed over from death to life, the Church invites her members, dispersed throughout the world, to gather in vigil and prayer. For this is the Passover of the Lord, in which, by hearing his Word and celebrating his Sacraments, we share in his victory over death.
>
> *The Celebrant may say the following prayer*
> Let us pray.
> O God, through your Son you have bestowed upon your people the brightness of your light: Sanctify this new fire, and grant that in this Paschal feast we may so burn with heavenly desires, that with pure minds we may attain to the festival of everlasting light; through Jesus Christ our Lord. *Amen.*

The Paschal Candle is then lighted from the newly kindled fire, and the Deacon (the Celebrant if there is no deacon) carrying the Candle, leads the procession to the chancel, pausing three times and singing or saying

                The light of Christ.
People   Thanks be to God.

If you have a candle, you will use the big paschal candle to light it. As your candle glows in the darkness, think of how the light of Jesus takes away the darkness in your life. Think of how Jesus wants us to bring light into the lives of our family and friends.

After the candles are lit, the Paschal Candle is placed in its stand in the chancel.

Now someone sings a very old song, the Exultet, that says we're thankful for the light of Christ that takes away our sins.

(The marked sections may be left out.)

    Rejoice now, heavenly hosts
      and choirs of angels,
    and let your trumpets shout Salvation
    for the victory of our mighty King.
    Rejoice and sing now, all the round earth,
    bright with a glorious splendor,
    for darkness has been vanquished
      by our eternal King.
    Rejoice and be glad now, Mother Church,
    and let your holy courts, in radiant light,
    resound with the praises of your people.

All you who stand near this marvelous
   and holy flame,
pray with me to God the Almighty
for the grace to sing the worthy praise
   of this great light;
through Jesus Christ his Son our Lord,
who lives and reigns with him,
in the unity of the Holy Spirit,
one God, for ever and ever. *Amen.*

	The Lord be with you.
Answer	And also with you.
Deacon	Let us give thanks to the Lord our God.
Answer	It is right to give him thanks and praise.

Deacon

It is truly right and good, always and everywhere, with our whole heart and mind and voice, to praise you, the invisible, almighty, and eternal God, and your only-begotten Son, Jesus Christ our Lord; for he is the true Paschal Lamb, who at the feast of the Passover paid for us the debt of Adam's sin, and by his blood delivered your faithful people.

This is the night, when you brought our fathers, the children of Israel, out of bondage in Egypt, and led them through the Red Sea on dry land.

This is the night, when all who believe in Christ are delivered from the gloom of sin, and are restored to grace and holiness of life.

This is the night, when Christ broke the bonds of death and hell, and rose victorious from the grave.

How wonderful and beyond our knowing, O God, is your mercy and loving-kindness to us, that to redeem a slave, you gave a Son.

How holy is this night, when wickedness is put to flight, and sin is washed away. It restores innocence to the fallen, and joy to those who mourn. It casts out pride and hatred, and brings peace and concord.

How blessed is this night, when earth and heaven are joined and man is reconciled to God.

Holy Father, accept our evening sacrifice, the offering of this candle in your honor. May it shine continually to drive away all darkness. May Christ, the Morning Star who knows no setting, find it ever burning—he who gives his light to all creation, and who lives and reigns for ever and ever. *Amen.*

It is customary for the Paschal Candle to burn at all services from Easter Day through the Day of Pentecost.

The Liturgy of the Word

One way we tell the story of Easter is to read from the Bible. These readings tell how God has always loved us and wanted us to be members of his family. Listen to what the celebrant reads, and learn what God has done to make us his people. Think of how much we can be thankful for.

Between each reading we may say or sing a song of praise. In some churches there might be a dance, another reading, or a short play between each lesson. In all these happy events we show how good we feel because God loves us so much.

The Celebrant may introduce the Scripture readings in these or similar words

Let us hear the record of God's saving deeds in history, how he saved his people in ages past; and let us pray that our God will bring each of us to the fullness of redemption.

At least two of the following Lessons are read, of which one is always the Lesson from Exodus. After each Lesson, the Psalm or Canticle listed, or some other suitable psalm, canticle, or hymn may be sung.

The story of Creation

Genesis 1:1—2:2; Psalm 33:1-11 or Psalm 36:5-10

Let us pray.   *(Silence)*

O God, who wonderfully created, and yet more wonderfully restored, the dignity of human nature: Grant that we may share the divine life of him who humbled himself to share our humanity, your Son Jesus Christ our Lord. *Amen.*

The Flood

Genesis 7:1-5, 11-18; 8:6-18; 9:8-13; Psalm 46

Let us pray.   *(Silence)*

Almighty God, you have placed in the skies the sign of your covenant with all living things: Grant that we, who are saved through water and the Spirit, may worthily offer to you our sacrifice of thanksgiving; through Jesus Christ our Lord. *Amen.*

Abraham's sacrifice of Isaac

Genesis 22:1-18; Psalm 33:12-22 or Psalm 16

Let us pray.   *(Silence)*

God and Father of all believers, for the glory of your Name multiply, by the grace of the sacrament, the number of your children; that your

Church may rejoice to see fulfilled your promise to our father Abraham; through Jesus Christ our Lord. *Amen.*

Israel's deliverance at the Red Sea

Exodus 14:10—15:1; Canticle 8, The Song of Moses

Let us pray.   *(Silence)*

O God, whose wonderful deeds of old shine forth even to our own day, you once delivered by the power of your mighty arm your chosen people from slavery under Pharaoh, to be a sign for us of the salvation of all nations by the water of Baptism: Grant that all the peoples of the earth may be numbered among the offspring of Abraham, and rejoice in the inheritance of Israel; through Jesus Christ our Lord. *Amen.*

God's Presence in a renewed Israel

Isaiah 4:2-6; Psalm 122

Let us pray.   *(Silence)*

O God, you led your ancient people by a pillar of cloud by day and a pillar of fire by night: Grant that we, who serve you now on earth, may come to the joy of that heavenly Jerusalem, where all tears are wiped away and where your saints for ever sing your praise; through Jesus Christ our Lord. *Amen.*

Salvation offered freely to all

Isaiah 55:1-11; Canticle 9, The First Song of Isaiah, or *Psalm 42:1-7*

Let us pray.   *(Silence)*

O God, you have created all things by the power of your Word, and you renew the earth by your Spirit: Give now the water of life to those who thirst for you, that they may bring forth abundant fruit in your glorious kingdom; through Jesus Christ our Lord. *Amen.*

A new heart and a new spirit
Ezekiel 36:24-28; Psalm 42:1-7,
or *Canticle 9, The First Song of Isaiah*

Let us pray. *(Silence)*

Almighty and everlasting God, who in the Paschal mystery established the new covenant of reconciliation: Grant that all who are reborn into the fellowship of Christ's Body may show forth in their lives what they profess by their faith; through Jesus Christ our Lord. *Amen.*

The valley of dry bones
Ezekiel 37:1-14; Psalm 30, or *Psalm 143*

Let us pray. *(Silence)*

Almighty God, by the Passover of your Son you have brought us out of sin into righteousness and out of death into life: Grant to those who are sealed by your Holy Spirit the will and the power to proclaim you to all the world; through Jesus Christ our Lord. *Amen.*

The gathering of God's people
Zephaniah 3:12-20; Psalm 98, or *Psalm 126*

Let us pray. *(Silence)*

O God of unchangeable power and eternal light: Look favorably on your whole Church, that wonderful and sacred mystery; by the effectual working of your providence, carry out in tranquillity the plan of salvation; let the whole world see and know that things which were cast down are being raised up, and things which had grown old are being made new, and that all things are being brought to their perfection by him through whom all things were made, your Son Jesus Christ our Lord. *Amen.*

Baptism and Renewal of Baptismal Vows

The paschal candle is lit after we hear the story of God's love for us, and each of us can now say "It's great to be part of God's family!" That's why Easter is a time to remember our baptism. Easter is also a wonderful time to baptize the people who haven't been baptized before.

To help you remember and prepare for renewing your baptismal vows, you may want to reread the story of Jimmy on page 3.

> *Holy Baptism (beginning with the Presentation of the Candidates and concluding with the reception of the newly baptized) may be administered here or after the Gospel. Confirmation may also be administered.*
>
> *In the absence of candidates for Baptism or Confirmation, the Celebrant leads the people in the Renewal of Baptismal Vows, either here or after the Gospel.*
>
> *The Celebrant may first address the people in these or similar words, all standing*

Through the Paschal mystery, dear friends, we are buried with Christ by Baptism into his death, and raised with him to newness of life. I call upon you, therefore, now that our Lenten observance is ended, to renew the solemn promises and vows of Holy Baptism, by which we once renounced Satan and all his works, and promised to serve God faithfully in his holy catholic Church.

Celebrant Do you reaffirm your renunciation of evil and renew your commitment to Jesus Christ?
People I do.

Celebrant Do you believe in God the Father?
People I believe in God, the Father almighty,
    creator of heaven and earth.

Celebrant Do you believe in Jesus Christ, the Son of God?
People I believe in Jesus Christ, his only Son, our Lord.
    He was conceived by the power
      of the Holy Spirit
      and born of the Virgin Mary.
    He suffered under Pontius Pilate,
      was crucified, died,
      and was buried.
    He descended to the dead.
    On the third day he rose again.
    He ascended into heaven,
      and is seated at the right hand
      of the Father.
    He will come again to judge the
      living and the dead.

Celebrant Do you believe in God the Holy Spirit?
People I believe in the Holy Spirit,
    the holy catholic Church,
    the communion of saints,
    the forgiveness of sins,
    the resurrection of the body,
    and the life everlasting.

Celebrant Will you continue in the apostles' teaching and fellowship, in the breaking of bread, and in the prayers?
People I will, with God's help.

Celebrant	Will you persevere in resisting evil, and, whenever you fall into sin, repent and return to the Lord?
People	I will, with God's help.
Celebrant	Will you proclaim by word and example the Good News of God in Christ?
People	I will, with God's help.
Celebrant	Will you seek and serve Christ in all persons, loving your neighbor as yourself?
People	I will, with God's help.
Celebrant	Will you strive for justice and peace among all people, and respect the dignity of every human being?
People	I will, with God's help.

The Celebrant concludes the Renewal of Vows as follows

May Almighty God, the Father of our Lord Jesus Christ, who has given us a new birth by water and the Holy Spirit, and bestowed upon us the forgiveness of sins, keep us in eternal life by his grace, in Christ Jesus our Lord. *Amen.*

At the Eucharist

Now we act out the story of Jesus being raised from the grave on Easter by sharing in the Holy Eucharist. Easter is the story behind the Eucharist. Look back on page 27 at the story of Tim and his sister Kathy. Remember that Kathy's mother gave of herself and that God gives us life through what Jesus did on Good Friday and Easter. We share in that gift every time we receive Holy Communion. So on Easter we participate in the Eucharist, and on every Sunday thereafter we can do the same thing.

The candles at the Altar may now be lighted from the Paschal Candle.

Immediately before the Canticle the Celebrant may say to the people

                Alleluia. Christ is risen.
People   The Lord is risen indeed. Alleluia.

One of the following Canticles is then sung:

                Gloria in excelsis
                Te Deum laudamus
                Pascha nostrum

The Celebrant then says

                The Lord be with you.
People   And also with you.
Celebrant   Let us pray.

The Celebrant says one of the following Collects

Almighty God, who for our redemption gave your only-begotten Son to the death of the cross, and by his glorious resurrection delivered us from the power of our enemy: Grant us so to die daily to sin, that we may evermore live with him in the joy of his resurrection; through Jesus Christ your Son our Lord, who lives and reigns with you and the Holy Spirit, one God, now and for ever. *Amen.*

or this

O God, who made this most holy night to shine with the glory of the Lord's resurrection: Stir up in your Church that Spirit of adoption which is given to us in Baptism, that we, being renewed both in body and mind, may worship you in sincerity and truth; through Jesus Christ our Lord, who lives and reigns with you, in the unity of the Holy Spirit, one God, now and for ever. *Amen.*

The Holy Eucharist continues on page 38.

Daily Morning Prayer

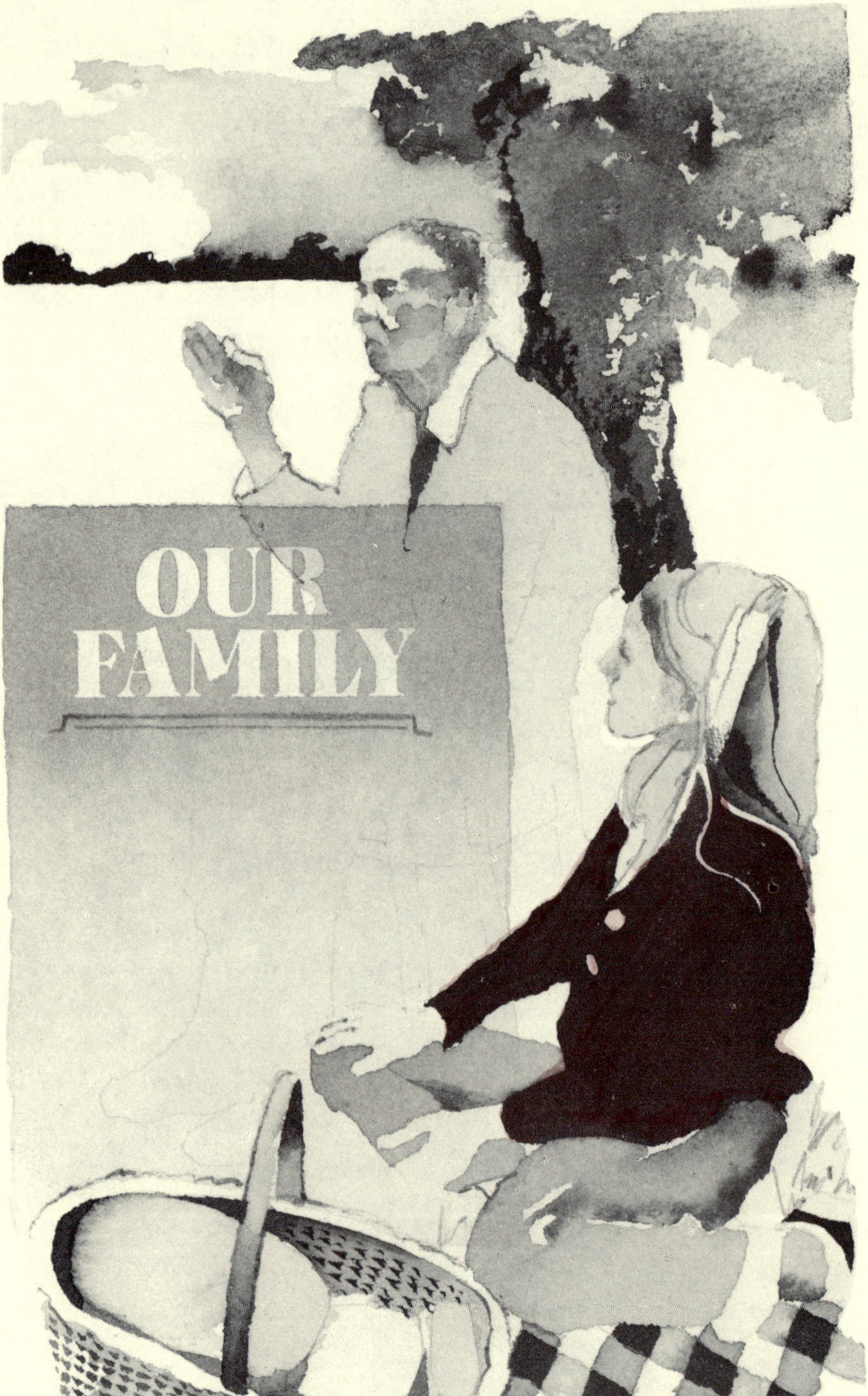
OUR
FAMILY

Mary was just about to go out the door when she heard her mother call to her. "Remember to ask Sue about the reunion Saturday. Don't forget!" Mary shifted her books from her left arm to her right. "Yeah," she said, "I'll remember."

As she walked to the corner where she always met her best friend, Mary thought about Saturday. Inviting Sue to the family reunion had been her mother's idea. "Since you're worried that you won't know anybody," her mother had said, "why not invite Sue?" Mary *was* worried. She could barely remember the last reunion five years ago. And even though she knew her aunts and uncles, there were many family members she couldn't remember at all. Inviting Sue seemed like a very good idea. At least they could talk to each other.

"It sounds like fun!" Sue said when Mary asked her. "Our family can't really have reunions," Sue explained, "since we're all so far apart. Besides three of my grandparents are dead." The rest of the way to school, the two girls talked about what Saturday would be like.

Everybody in Mary's family got up early that Saturday. The reunion was going to be in Redwood Falls, nearly one hundred miles away, and Mary's parents wanted to get an early start to avoid the hot September sun. "I'm here," Sue called out as she came in the back door. Within minutes Mary and Sue and Mike, Mary's younger brother, were in the back seat, and Mary's mom and dad and her older brother, Peter, were in the front. During the ride they exchanged stories about some of the people who were coming to Redwood Falls. By the time they arrived, Mary was looking forward to the rest of the day.

After only an hour, they all sat down to a picnic lunch that was spread out on tables underneath a huge oak tree. Mary and Sue listened as Mary's grandfather said grace—a long and very beautiful prayer that mentioned all his brothers and sisters. When they began to eat, Sue asked about the prayer. "It was written by his father," Peter said. "He says it as grace for every reunion. Most of the adults here probably know it by heart."

By the end of the day Mary and Sue were so tired they could hardly hold up their heads for the drive home. There had been singing and much story-telling. Then Mary's great-uncle Tony had gotten up in front of everybody and made a speech about the family. He talked about what various family members were doing, who was going to college, who had new babies, who had died. Then he said, "Here, I've got enough of these for everybody," and he passed out some booklets he'd made. "Our Family" was printed across the front of the booklets, and inside there was a family tree showing how everyone was related to everyone else. He had listed all their names and addresses and had even included the recipe for Aunt Nellie's baked beans.

On the way home Mary took out the booklet. She leafed through the pages as her mother drove. They were sitting next to each other in the front seat, with Sue next to the window, fast asleep. "You know, Mom," she said, "this booklet took a lot of work." Her mother smiled. "I'm sure it did," she agreed. "Tony does it for every reunion, and I think his father did it before him."

Mary was quiet. Now I know why the day was so special, she thought to herself. People were doing things they had done many times before—all to celebrate their membership in a family of many, many people, old and young. Mary liked the way her mother knew just what to expect—her grandfather's prayer, all the familiar songs, the speech Uncle Tony gave. Mary knew she would remember this day, and the next time she went to a reunion, it would all be familiar to her too. It would be a day to look forward to.

Going to church is something like Mary's family reunion. In church we remember and celebrate our membership in God's family. When we go to Morning Prayer, we are joining with other members of God's family to sing and pray and, sometimes, to listen to a sermon. Just as Sue and Mary learned more about Mary's family by listening to the storytelling, singing songs, and hearing Uncle Tony's speech, we can learn about God's family by sharing in Morning Prayer.

Morning Prayer is a very old service. In many religious communities, such as monasteries, convents, and seminaries, Morning Prayer is said every day. And just as Mary's mother looked forward to her family reunion, we can look forward to celebrating our membership in God's family at Morning Prayer.

Morning Prayer is different from baptism or Holy Eucharist because we don't act out anything during it. Instead, we pray and listen and sing. When we are baptized, we go under the water and come up again to act out the death and resurrection of Jesus. During Holy Communion we act out his death and resurrection again by doing what he taught us at the Last Supper. At Morning Prayer we sing and pray with our heavenly Father. We are getting to know him better.

The custom of Morning Prayer started long ago with some of the early followers of Jesus who gathered together at dawn and at sunset to pray, to sing, and to read Scripture and other religious material. Monasteries and convents soon began to hold these services, not only in the morning and evening but also at the third, sixth, and ninth hours of the day, and then again at midnight. But this practice of daily prayer goes back even further. It has its roots in the Jewish tradition of praising and remembering God at fixed hours of the day.

Just as our ancestors used daily prayer as a time to share and express their beliefs together, we too can participate in Morning and Evening Prayer. Both of these services are included in *The Book of Common Prayer*. When we use them, we are not only remembering God but we are also remembering members of the family of God who lived long before us.

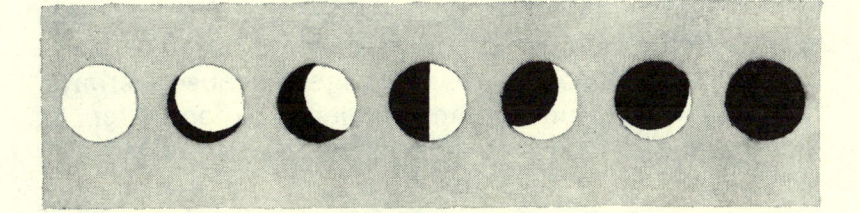

The Church Calendar

We keep calendars to remind us of important occasions we don't want to forget. In this way the church calendar is like our regular yearly calendar. On the fourth of July we have Independence Day to remind us that our freedom is important. On the first Monday in September we have Labor Day to honor the hard work of those who make our lives better. The church calendar works the same way. It reminds us of important events and people in the history of the family of God.

The church calendar is divided into seasons. These seasons are based on traditions that began long before the time of Jesus, when ancient people counted the passage of time by watching the cycles of the sun or the phases of the moon. A calendar based on the moon, like the Hebrew calendar, has thirteen months in it. A calendar based on the sun, like the Roman calendar and like our own calendar today, has twelve months in it. The church calendar comes from both the Hebrew and the Roman traditions, so it is based partly on the changes in the moon and partly on the changes in the sun.

Christmas gets its date from the sun. At the time of the early church, the winter solstice—when the sun appears for the shortest time—occurred on December 25. People thought of that day as the birth of the sun because it appeared to grow bigger afterward. So the church chose that day to celebrate the birth of its "sun," Jesus.

Easter gets its date from the moon, and it changes every year. Like the Hebrew calendar, Easter is based on the phases of the moon: its date changes because it always falls on the first Sunday after the first full moon after March 21. The Passover, an ancient Jewish festival, is also celebrated at the same time.

The church year begins with Advent, a time of waiting for the birth of Jesus. During this season we remember the yearning of the Jewish people as they waited for their Messiah. The word *Advent* comes from a Latin word that means *coming*.

Epiphany is the season that comes right after Christmas. Its name comes from a Greek word that means *showing*. During Epiphany we celebrate the great gift that God gave us in sending his son.

The season that prepares us for Easter is called Lent. During Lent we remember our sins, and then on Easter we celebrate the new life we have received through the resurrection of Jesus.

The Bible tells us that forty days after Jesus was raised from the dead, he was taken up into heaven. Christians celebrate this event on Ascension Day, which always comes on a Thursday.

The Bible tells us about an amazing event that happened ten days after the ascension. On this day, when the disciples were gathered together for a Jewish harvest festival, the Holy Spirit visited them in a special way that was very powerful. The visit caused the disciples to feel greater love and understanding than they had before. We call this visit of the Holy Spirit "Pentecost," from the Greek word *pentēkonta,* meaning *fifty*. We celebrate Pentecost fifty days after the resurrection of Jesus.

The church calendar also celebrates special days. This tradition began in very early times when the Church remembered its heroes by celebrating the day of their death, which is also the day of their birth in heaven. We remember Saint Paul, for example, on January 25, Saint Joseph on March 19, and Saint Mary on August 15.

Years later the Church also began to remember events in Jesus' life on certain days. We celebrate the Annunciation of the Archangel Gabriel to Mary on March 25, the Transfiguration of Jesus on August 6, and the Holy Cross on September 14.

Occasionally we celebrate an important teaching of the Church, so, for example, we have Trinity Sunday on the Sunday after Pentecost.

Notice how each Bible quotation for beginning Morning Prayer tells you something about the seasons of the church year.

What Happens at Daily Morning Prayer

The Beginning
Confession of Sin
The Invitatory and Psalter
The Lessons
The Canticles (Songs 8-21)
The Apostles' Creed
The Prayers
The Suffrages
The Collects
The Ending

The Beginning

The opening sentence of Daily Morning Prayer tells where we are in the church season. Since the church calendar begins with Advent, the first Bible quotation for Morning Prayer is for the season of Advent. You can follow the order of the church calendar by looking at the seasonal choices for the opening of Morning Prayer.

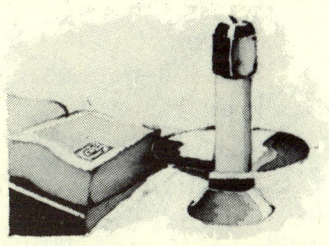

The Officiant begins the service with one or more of these sentences of Scripture, or with the versicle "Lord, open our lips" on page 130.

Advent

Watch, for you do not know when the master of the house will come, in the evening, or at midnight, or at cockcrow, or in the morning, lest he come suddenly and find you asleep.
Mark 13:35,36

In the wilderness prepare the way of the Lord, make straight in the desert a highway for our God. *Isaiah 40:3*

The glory of the Lord shall be revealed, and all flesh shall see it together. *Isaiah 40:5*

Christmas

Behold, I bring you good news of a great joy which will come to all the people; for to you is born this day in the city of David, a Savior, who is Christ the Lord. *Luke 2:10,11*

Behold, the dwelling of God is with mankind. He will dwell with them, and they shall be his people, and God himself will be with them, and be their God. *Revelation 21:3*

Epiphany

Nations shall come to your light, and kings to the brightness of your rising. *Isaiah 60:3*

I will give you as a light to the nations, that my salvation may reach to the end of the earth.
Isaiah 49:6b

From the rising of the sun to its setting my Name shall be great among the nations, and in every place incense shall be offered to my Name, and a pure offering; for my Name shall be great among the nations, says the Lord of hosts.
Malachi 1:11

Lent

If we say we have no sin, we deceive ourselves, and the truth is not in us, but if we confess our sins, God, who is faithful and just, will forgive our sins and cleanse us from all unrighteousness.
1 John 1:8, 9

Rend your hearts and not your garments. Return to the Lord your God, for he is gracious and merciful, slow to anger and abounding in steadfast love, and repents of evil. *Joel 2:13*

I will arise and go to my father, and I will say to him, "Father, I have sinned against heaven and before you; I am no longer worthy to be called your son." *Luke 15:18, 19*

To the Lord our God belong mercy and forgiveness, because we have rebelled against him and have not obeyed the voice of the Lord our God by following his laws which he set before us.
Daniel 9:9, 10

Jesus said, "If anyone would come after me, let him deny himself and take up his cross and follow me." *Mark 8:34*

Holy Week

All we like sheep have gone astray; we have turned every one to his own way; and the Lord has laid on him the iniquity of us all. *Isaiah 53:6*

Is it nothing to you, all you who pass by? Look and see if there is any sorrow like my sorrow which was brought upon me, whom the Lord has afflicted. *Lamentations 1:12*

Easter Season, including Ascension Day and the Day of Pentecost

Alleluia! Christ is risen.
The Lord is risen indeed. Alleluia!

On this day the Lord has acted; we will rejoice and be glad in it. *Psalm 118:24*

Thanks be to God, who gives us the victory through our Lord Jesus Christ. *1 Corinthians 15:57*

If then you have been raised with Christ, seek the things that are above, where Christ is, seated at the right hand of God. *Colossians 3:1*

Christ has entered, not into a sanctuary made with hands, a copy of the true one, but into heaven itself, now to appear in the presence of God on our behalf. *Hebrews 9:24*

You shall receive power when the Holy Spirit has come upon you; and you shall be my witnesses in Jerusalem, and in all Judea, and Samaria, and to the ends of the earth. *Acts 1:8*

Trinity Sunday

Holy, holy, holy is the Lord God Almighty, who was, and is, and is to come! *Revelation 4:8*

All Saints and other Major Saints' Days

We give thanks to the Father, who has made us worthy to share in the inheritance of the saints in light. *Colossians 1:12*

You are no longer strangers and sojourners, but fellow citizens with the saints and members of the household of God. *Ephesians 2:19*

Their sound has gone out into all lands, and their message to the ends of the world. *Psalm 19:4*

Occasions of Thanksgiving

Give thanks to the Lord, and call upon his Name; make known his deeds among the peoples. *Psalm 105:1*

At any Time

Grace to you and peace from God our Father and the Lord Jesus Christ. *Philippians 1:2*

I was glad when they said to me, "Let us go to the house of the Lord." *Psalm 122:1*

Let the words of my mouth and the meditation of my heart be acceptable in your sight, O Lord, my strength and my redeemer. *Psalm 19:14*

Send out your light and your truth, that they may lead me, and bring me to your holy hill and to your dwelling. *Psalm 43:3*

The Lord is in his holy temple; let all the earth keep silence before him. *Habakkuk 2:20*

The hour is coming, and now is, when the true worshipers will worship the Father in spirit and truth, for such the Father seeks to worship him. *John 4:23*

Thus says the high and lofty One who inhabits eternity, whose name is Holy, "I dwell in the high and holy place and also with the one who has a contrite and humble spirit, to revive the spirit of the humble and to revive the heart of the contrite." *Isaiah 57:15*

Confession of Sin

We begin with a confession. We don't say out loud what we've done wrong, but we say that we know we feel separated from God and that we want to be close to him again. We say this right at the beginning because it's hard to hear God's story and to sing to him as long as we feel far away from him. We need to admit our feeling of separation to God. Then the priest assures us that God forgives us. When we are forgiven, we can be closer to God and to each other.

The following Confession of Sin may then be said; or the liturgy may continue at once with "Lord, open our lips."

The Officiant says to the people

Dearly beloved, we have come together in the presence of Almighty God our heavenly Father, to set forth his praise, to hear his holy Word, and to ask, for ourselves and on behalf of others, those things that are necessary for our life and our salvation. And so that we may prepare ourselves in heart and mind to worship him, let us kneel in silence, and with penitent and obedient hearts confess our sins, that we may obtain forgiveness by his infinite goodness and mercy.

or this

Let us confess our sins against God and our neighbor.

Silence may be kept.

Officiant and People together, all kneeling

Most merciful God,
we confess that we have sinned against you
in thought, word, and deed,
by what we have done,
and by what we have left undone.

We have not loved you with our whole heart;
we have not loved our neighbors as ourselves.
We are truly sorry and we humbly repent.
For the sake of your Son Jesus Christ,
have mercy on us and forgive us;
that we may delight in your will,
and walk in your ways,
to the glory of your Name. Amen.

The Priest alone stands and says

Almighty God have mercy on you, forgive you all your sins through our Lord Jesus Christ, strengthen you in all goodness, and by the power of the Holy Spirit keep you in eternal life. *Amen.*

A deacon or lay person using the above form remains kneeling, and substitutes "us" for "you" and "our" for "your."

The Invitatory and Psalter

A versicle is a very short prayer spoken by the officiant. The people always respond to the versicle. This response is called the doxology. It is also sometimes called the *Gloria Patri* (which means *glory to the father*) because these are the first two words of the doxology in Latin. This prayer is a very ancient praise of God.

When early Christians got together for daily prayer, their service began when the leader said "Lord, open our lips." These words ask God to let our very first words of the day be words that praise him.

All stand

Officiant	Lord, open our lips.
People	And our mouth shall proclaim your praise.

Then we say some very old Christian words that praise God. These words say that we, as Christians, know God in three ways. We know him as a loving parent who gives us life. We know him as a son who is like us and who shows us that God loves us. We know him as a spirit that is like a great and powerful wind, moving us to become like God.

Officiant and People

Glory to the Father, and to the Son, and to the Holy Spirit: as it was in the beginning, is now, and will be for ever. Amen.

Except in Lent, add Alleluia.

We sing some Old Testament songs, or sometimes we say the words instead of singing them. These songs remind us that Christians and Jews share a common past. These songs are psalms. The first is an invitatory psalm, because it invites us to worship. On certain seasonal or special days, additional words are sung or said before and after the invitatory psalm. These *antiphons* are musical verses which remind us of the message of the season.

One of the following Antiphons may be sung or said with the Invitatory Psalm.

In Advent

Our King and Savior now draws near: Come let us adore him.

In Christmas Season

Alleluia. To us a child is born: Come let us adore him. Alleluia.

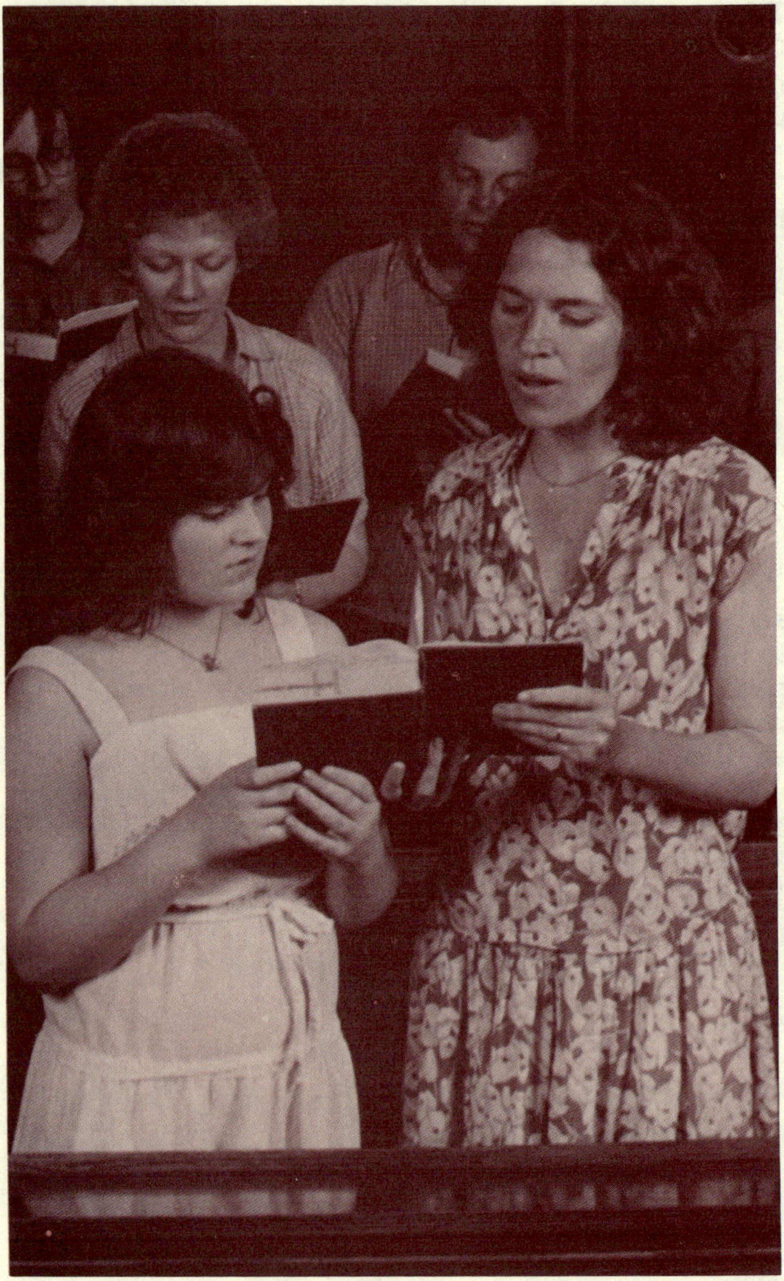

From the Epiphany through the Baptism of Christ, and on the Feasts of the Transfiguration and Holy Cross

The Lord has shown forth his glory: Come let us adore him.

In Lent

The Lord is full of compassion and mercy: Come let us adore him.

From Easter Day until the Ascension

Alleluia. The Lord is risen indeed: Come let us adore him. Alleluia.

From Ascension Day until the Day of Pentecost

Alleluia. Christ the Lord has ascended into heaven: Come let us adore him. Alleluia.

On the Day of Pentecost

Alleluia. The Spirit of the Lord renews the face of the earth: Come let us adore him. Alleluia.

On Trinity Sunday

Father, Son, and Holy Spirit, one God: Come let us adore him.

On other Sundays and weekdays

The earth is the Lord's, for he made it: Come let us adore him.

or this

Worship the Lord in the beauty of holiness: Come let us adore him.

or this

The mercy of the Lord is everlasting: Come let us adore him.

The Alleluias in the following Antiphons are used only in Easter Season.

On Feasts of the Incarnation

[Alleluia.] The Word was made flesh and dwelt among us: Come let us adore him. [Alleluia.]

On All Saints and other Major Saints' Days

[Alleluia.] The Lord is glorious in his saints: Come let us adore him. [Alleluia.]

Then follows one of the Invitatory Psalms, Venite or Jubilate.

Venite   *Psalm 95:1-7*

Come, let us sing to the Lord;*
   let us shout for joy to the Rock
     of our salvation.
Let us come before his presence
     with thanksgiving*
   and raise a loud shout to him
     with psalms.
For the Lord is a great God,*
   and a great King above all gods.
In his hand are the caverns of the earth,*
   and the heights of the hills are his also.
The sea is his, for he made it,*
   and his hands have molded
     the dry land.
Come, let us bow down,
     and bend the knee,*
   and kneel before the Lord our Maker.
For he is our God,
and we are the people of his pasture
     and the sheep of his hand,*
     Oh, that today you would hearken
       to his voice!

or Psalm 95 may be used instead.

Jubilate   Psalm 100

Be joyful in the Lord, all you lands;*
  serve the Lord with gladness
  and come before his presence
    with a song.
Know this: The Lord himself is God;*
  he himself has made us, and we are his;
  we are his people and the sheep
    of his pasture.
Enter his gates with thanksgiving;
go into his courts with praise;*
  give thanks to him and call
    upon his Name.
For the Lord is good;
his mercy is everlasting;*
  and his faithfulness endures
    from age to age.

The one time in the church year that we don't use an invitatory psalm from the Old Testament is from Easter Sunday until seven weeks later, on Pentecost Sunday. Pentecost is the day when we remember the time the Holy Spirit came to the apostles as a powerful wind and a cleansing fire. You can read about Pentecost in Acts 2:1-4. We don't use an Old Testament psalm during this time because we want to praise God especially for sending his son to die and to be raised from the grave for us. Even though we share a common heritage with the Jews, Christians are different from the Jews because Christians believe that we must know Jesus in order to know God. We believe that Jesus is different from all other humans.

So from Easter to Pentecost we praise God by singing words from the New Testament that give thanks for Jesus' resurrection.

Christ our Passover   *Pascha nostrum*

1 Corinthians 5:7-8; Romans 6:9-11; 1 Corinthians 15:20-22

Alleluia.
Christ our Passover has been sacrificed
    for us;*
  therefore let us keep the feast,
Not with the old leaven, the leaven
    of malice and evil,*
  but with the unleavened bread
    of sincerity and truth. Alleluia.

Christ being raised from the dead
    will never die again;*
  death no longer has dominion over him.
The death that he died, he died to sin,
    once for all;*
  but the life he lives, he lives to God.
So also consider yourselves dead to sin,*
  and alive to God in Jesus Christ
    our Lord. Alleluia.

Christ has been raised from the dead,*
  the first fruits of those who have
    fallen asleep.
For since by a man came death,*
  by a man has come also the resurrection
    of the dead.
For as in Adam all die,*
  so also in Christ shall all be made alive.
    Alleluia.

After the Old Testament psalm inviting us to worship, or the verses praising Jesus' resurrection, we usually read psalms from the Old Testament. This reading is between the leader and the people in church or, sometimes, between the people on different sides of the aisle. The psalms were the Church's first song book, and sometimes we still sing them.

> *At the end of the Psalms is sung or said*
> Glory to the Father, and to the Son, and to the
>   Holy Spirit:*
> as it was in the beginning, is now,
>   and will be for ever. Amen.

The Lessons

This is the second part of Morning Prayer. We begin by listening to readings from the Bible. There may be two or three selections.

> *One or two selected Lessons are read, the Reader first saying*
> A Reading (Lesson) from _____ .
>
> *A citation giving chapter and verse of the Scripture may be added.*
> *After each Lesson the Reader may say*
>   The Word of the Lord.
> *Answer*   Thanks be to God.
> *Or the Reader may say*
>   Here ends the Lesson (Reading).
>
> *Silence may be kept after each Reading.*

The Canticles

Telling the story of God and his people and singing the songs about the family of God are just like Sue's and Mary's experience at the family reunion: they and the rest of Mary's family were all telling stories and singing songs. We come to know the meaning of God's family so much better when we do these things together.

We sing a song, called a *canticle,* after each Bible reading. Together, these canticles make a little Christian songbook. The first is number 8, because the big prayer book has other versions that are numbered 1 through 7.

Some of these songs come from the Old Testament, some from the New Testament, and some from the part of the Bible which, in the Episcopal church, is in between the Old and New Testaments. It is called the *Apocrypha.* Two of these songs were written in the very early Church and are not in the Bible at all.

Songs 8, 9, 10, 11 are from the Old Testament. In Song 8 Moses thanks God for leading the Hebrews safely through the Red Sea while all the Egyptian soldiers drowned. This is a song of thanksgiving to God for freeing the Hebrews.

8 The Song of Moses   *Cantemus Domino*
Exodus 15:1-6, 11-13, 17-18

I will sing to the Lord, for he is lofty
    and uplifted;*
  the horse and its rider has he hurled
    into the sea.
The Lord is my strength and my refuge;*
  the Lord has become my Savior.
This is my God and I will praise him,*

the God of my people and I will
  exalt him.
The Lord is a mighty warrior;*
  Yahweh is his Name.
The chariots of Pharaoh and his army
    has he hurled into the sea;*
  the finest of those who bear armor
    have been drowned in the Red Sea.
The fathomless deep has
    overwhelmed them;*
  they sank into the depths like a stone.
Your right hand, O Lord, is glorious in might;*
  your right hand, O Lord, has overthrown
    the enemy.
Who can be compared with you, O Lord,
    among the gods?*
  who is like you, glorious in holiness,
  awesome in renown, and worker
    of wonders?
You stretched forth your right hand;*
  the earth swallowed them up.
With your constant love you led
    the people you redeemed;*
  with your might you brought them
    in safety to your holy dwelling.
You will bring them in and plant them*
  on the mount of your possession,
The resting-place you have made
    for yourself, O Lord,*
  the sanctuary, O Lord, that your hand
    has established.
The Lord shall reign*
  for ever and for ever.
Glory to the Father, and to the Son,
    and to the Holy Spirit:*
  as it was in the beginning, is now,
    and will be for ever. Amen.

Song 9 is a song of thanksgiving which includes the words of a prophet, Isaiah, who lived seven hundred years before Jesus. In this song, Isaiah has just predicted that God will help the Hebrews defeat all their enemies.

9 The First Song of Isaiah *Ecce, Deus*
Isaiah 12:2-6

Surely, it is God who saves me;*
  I will trust in him and not be afraid.
For the Lord is my stronghold and my
    sure defense,*
  and he will be my Savior.
Therefore you shall draw water
    with rejoicing*
  from the springs of salvation.
And on that day you shall say,*
  Give thanks to the Lord and call
    upon his Name;
Make his deeds known among the peoples;*
  see that they remember that his Name
    is exalted.
Sing the praises of the Lord, for he has
    done great things,*
  and this is known in all the world.
Cry aloud, inhabitants of Zion,
    ring out your joy,*
  for the great one in the midst of you
    is the Holy One of Israel.

Glory to the Father, and to the Son,
    and to the Holy Spirit:*
  as it was in the beginning, is now,
    and will be for ever. Amen.

Although Song 10 is also called a song of Isaiah, it was probably written by someone who lived 150 years after

Isaiah. In the song, the Jews have been defeated by a foreign power, and the singer is telling what they should do to return to their homeland.

10   The Second Song of Isaiah   *Quaerite Dominum*

Isaiah 55:6-11

Seek the Lord while he wills to be found;*
 call upon him when he draws near.
Let the wicked forsake their ways*
 and the evil ones their thoughts;
And let them turn to the Lord,
  and he will have compassion,*
 and to our God, for he will
  richly pardon.
For my thoughts are not your thoughts,*
 nor your ways my ways, says the Lord.
For as the heavens are higher
  than the earth,*
 so are my ways higher than your ways,
 and my thoughts than your thoughts.
For as rain and snow fall from the heavens*
 and return not again, but water the earth,
Bringing forth life and giving growth,*
 seed for sowing and bread for eating,
So is my word that goes forth from
  my mouth;*
 it will not return to me empty;
But it will accomplish that which
  I have purposed,*
 and prosper in that for which I sent it.

Glory to the Father, and to the Son,
  and to the Holy Spirit:*
 as it was in the beginning, is now,
  and will be for ever. Amen.

Like Song 10, this song is from the book of the prophet Isaiah, but it was probably written by someone two hundred years after Isaiah. This is a happy song in which the author foresees God bringing the Jewish people back to their homeland.

11 The Third Song of Isaiah   *Surge, illuminare*
Isaiah 60:1-3, 11a, 14c, 18-19

Arise, shine, for your light has come,*
   and the glory of the Lord
     has dawned upon you.
For behold, darkness covers the land;*
   deep gloom enshrouds the peoples.
But over you the Lord will rise,*
   and his glory will appear upon you.
Nations will stream to your light,*
   and kings to the brightness of
     your dawning.
Your gates will always be open;*
   by day or night they will never be shut.
They will call you, The City of the Lord,*
   The Zion of the Holy One of Israel.
Violence will no more be heard in your land,*
   ruin or destruction within your borders.
You will call your walls, Salvation,*
   and all your portals, Praise.
The sun will no more be your light by day;*
   by night you will not need the brightness
     of the moon.
The Lord will be your everlasting light,*
   and your God will be your glory.

Glory to the Father, and to the Son,
   and to the Holy Spirit:*
     as it was in the beginning, is now,
       and will be for ever. Amen.

Songs 12, 13, and 14 come from the Apocrypha. The first two songs are attributed to the "three young men." In the Old Testament's Book of Daniel, there is a story about three young men who wouldn't worship an idol made by a foreign king. They only wanted to worship God. This made the king so angry that he threw them into a fire. Instead of dying, these three men got up and walked around, right in the fire. God protected them. Songs 12 and 13 are about what these men sang while they were in the fire.

An invocation, as it's used in Song 12, means an introductory prayer, asking God to listen to us.

12   A Song of Creation   *Benedicite, omnia opera Domini*

Song of the Three Young Men, 35-65

One or more sections of this Canticle may be used. Whatever the selection, it begins with the Invocation and concludes with the Doxology.

Invocation

Glorify the Lord, all you works
    of the Lord,*
  praise him and highly exalt him
    for ever.
In the firmament of his power, glorify
    the Lord,*
  Praise him and highly exalt
    him for ever.

I The Cosmic Order

Glorify the Lord, you angels and all
    powers of the Lord,*
  O heavens and all waters above
    the heavens.

Sun and moon and stars of the sky,
>   glorify the Lord,*
> praise him and highly exalt him for ever.

Glorify the Lord, every shower of rain
>   and fall of dew,*
> all winds and fire and heat.

Winter and summer, glorify the Lord,*
> praise him and highly exalt him for ever.

Glorify the Lord, O chill and cold,*
> drops of dew and flakes of snow.

Frost and cold, ice and sleet,
>   glorify the Lord,*
> praise him and highly exalt him for ever.

Glorify the Lord, O nights and days,*
> O shining light and enfolding dark.

Storm clouds and thunderbolts,
>   glorify the Lord,*
> praise him and highly exalt him for ever.

II The Earth and its Creatures

Let the earth glorify the Lord,*
> praise him and highly exalt him for ever.

Glorify the Lord, O mountains and hills,
and all that grows upon the earth,*
> praise him and highly exalt him for ever.

Glorify the Lord, O springs of water,
>   seas, and streams,*
> O whales and all that move in the waters.

All birds of the air, glorify the Lord,*
> praise him and highly exalt him for ever.

Glorify the Lord, O beasts of the wild,*
and all you flocks and herds.

O men and women everywhere, glorify
>   the Lord,*
> praise him and highly exalt him for ever.

III The People of God

Let the people of God glorify the Lord,*
    praise him and highly exalt him for ever.
Glorify the Lord, O priests and
        servants of the Lord,*
    praise him and highly exalt him for ever.
Glorify the Lord, O spirits and souls
        of the righteous,*
    praise him and highly exalt him for ever.
You that are holy and humble of heart,
        glorify the Lord,*
    praise him and highly exalt him for ever.

Doxology

Let us glorify the Lord: Father, Son,
        and Holy Spirit;*
    praise him and highly exalt him for ever.
In the firmament of his power,
        glorify the Lord,*
    praise him and highly exalt him for ever.

13 A Song of Praise   *Benedictus es, Domine*
Song of the Three Young Men, 29-34

Glory to you, Lord God of our fathers;*
    you are worthy of praise; glory to you.

Glory to you for the radiance of your holy Name;*
    we will praise you and highly exalt you for ever.

Glory to you in the splendor of your temple;*
    on the throne of your majesty, glory to you.

Glory to you, seated between the Cherubim;*
    we will praise you and highly exalt you for ever.

Glory to you, beholding the depths;*
    in the high vault of heaven, glory to you.
Glory to you, Father, Son, and Holy Spirit;*
    we will praise You and highly exalt you for ever.

Manasseh was a king over the Hebrews. During the first part of his rule he was a very bad king. He made everyone worship idols. Then God sent foreign armies to punish him. Afterward, Manasseh repented and was sorry. During the later part of his rule, he was a good king. Much later, someone remembered Manasseh and wrote a song about his repentance. This is Song 14.

14   A Song of Penitence   *Kyrie Pantokrator*
Prayer of Manasseh, 1-2, 4, 6-7, 11-15

Especially suitable in Lent, and on other penitential occasions

O Lord and Ruler of the hosts of heaven,*
    God of Abraham, Isaac, and Jacob,
    and of all their righteous offspring:
You made the heavens and the earth,*
    with all their vast array.
All things quake with fear at your presence;*
    they tremble because of your power.
But your merciful promise is beyond
        all measure;*
    it surpasses all that our minds can fathom.
O Lord, you are full of compassion,*
    long-suffering, and abounding in mercy.
You hold back your hand;*
    you do not punish as we deserve.
In your great goodness, Lord,
you have promised forgiveness to sinners,*
    that they may repent of their sin
    and be saved.

And now, O Lord, I bend the knee
  of my heart,*
 and make my appeal, sure of your
  gracious goodness.
I have sinned, O Lord, I have sinned,*
 and I know my wickedness only too well.
Therefore I make this prayer to you:*
 Forgive me, Lord, forgive me.
Do not let me perish in my sin,*
 nor condemn me to the depths
  of the earth.
For you, O Lord, are the God of those
  who repent,*
 and in me you will show forth
  your goodness.
Unworthy as I am, you will save me,
in accordance with your great mercy,*
 and I will praise you without ceasing
  all the days of my life.
For all the powers of heaven
  sing your praises,*
 and yours is the glory to ages
  of ages. Amen.

Songs 15, 16, 17, 18, and 19 are from the New Testament. The first three of these are from Luke's Gospel. When the Archangel Gabriel came to Mary and told her that she would be the mother of Jesus, Mary sang a song of thanksgiving and praise.

15   The Song of Mary   *Magnificat*
Luke 1:46-55

My soul proclaims the greatness
  of the Lord,
my spirit rejoices in God my Savior;*
 for he has looked with favor on his
  lowly servant.

From this day all generations will call
    me blessed:*
  the Almighty has done great things
    for me,
  and holy is his Name.
He has mercy on those who fear him*
  in every generation.
He has shown the strength of his arm,*
  he has scattered the proud
    in their conceit.
He has cast down the mighty
    from their thrones,*
  and has lifted up the lowly.
He has filled the hungry with good things,*
  and the rich he has sent away empty.
He has come to the help of his
    servant Israel,*
  for he has remembered his promise
    of mercy,
The promise he made to our fathers,*
  to Abraham and his children for ever.

Glory to the Father, and to the Son,
    and to the Holy Spirit:*
  as it was in the beginning, is now,
    and will be for ever. Amen.

Zechariah was a priest of the Jewish Temple, and his wife, Elizabeth, was Mary's cousin. The Archangel Gabriel came to Zechariah and told him that Elizabeth would have a baby and that the baby should be named John. Zechariah didn't believe the angel. Because he didn't believe, he was punished by losing his ability to speak. After Elizabeth had her baby, the neighbors came to visit. They asked Zechariah what the baby should be named. Suddenly Zechariah could speak again! "John," he said.

Then he sang this song, which is Number 16. The song describes how God sent Zechariah's son, John the Baptist, to announce the coming of Jesus.

16 The Song of Zechariah *Benedictus Dominus Deus*

Luke 1:68-79

Blessed be the Lord, the God of Israel;*
    he has come to his people
        and set them free.
He has raised up for us a mighty savior,*
    born of the house of his servant David.
Through his holy prophets he promised
        of old,
that he would save us from our enemies,*
    from the hands of all who hate us.
He promised to show mercy to our fathers*
    and to remember his holy covenant.
This was the oath he swore to our
        father Abraham,*
    to set us free from the hands
        of our enemies,
Free to worship him without fear,*
    holy and righteous in his sight
        all the days of our life.
You, my child, shall be called the prophet
        of the Most High,*
    for you will go before the Lord
        to prepare his way,
To give his people knowledge of salvation*
    by the forgiveness of their sins.
In the tender compassion of our God*
    the dawn from on high shall break
        upon us,
To shine on those who dwell in darkness
    and the shadow of death,*
    and to guide our feet into the way of peace.

Glory to the Father, and to the Son,
> and to the Holy Spirit:*
>> as it was in the beginning, is now,
>> and will be for ever. Amen.

There was a very old and very holy man whose name was Simeon. He spent all his time in the Jewish Temple in Jerusalem. Simeon believed that God promised him he wouldn't die until he had seen the person God sent to free the Jews. The Jews had a custom of bringing the first son to the Temple to give thanks to God for his birth. When Joseph and Mary brought the baby Jesus to the Temple, Simeon knew instantly that God's promise had been fulfilled. This is his song of thanksgiving.

17 The Song of Simeon   *Nunc dimittis*
Luke 2:29-32

Lord, you now have set your servant free*
> to go in peace as you have promised;

For these eyes of mine have seen
>> the Savior,*
>> whom you have prepared for all
>> the world to see:

A Light to enlighten the nations,*
> and the glory of your people Israel.

Glory to the Father, and to the Son,
> and to the Holy Spirit:*
>> as it was in the beginning, is now,
>> and will be for ever. Amen.

Songs 18 and 19 are by a man named John who was a prisoner on the island of Patmos. John was imprisoned because he was a Christian at a time when it was against the law to practice Christianity. While he was on the island, John had a series of visions. Song 18 is about one of John's visions. He sees Jesus as a lamb surrounded by the family of God. To the Jews of that time, the lamb stood for gifts we offer to God.

18   A Song to the Lamb   *Dignus es*
Revelation 4:11; 5:9-10, 13

Splendor and honor and kingly power*
 are yours by right, O Lord our God,
For you created everything that is,*
 and by your will they were created
  and have their being;
And yours by right, O Lamb that
  was slain,*
 for with your blood you have redeemed
  for God,
From every family, language, people,
  and nation,*
 a kingdom of priests to serve our God.

And so, to him who sits upon the throne,*
 and to Christ the Lamb,
Be worship and praise, dominion
  and splendor,*
 for ever and for evermore.

Song 19 is about another one of John's visions. Here John sees the end of the world. He sees some people with God, and others who are separated from God and destroyed. This song is sung by the people who are with God.

19   The Song of the Redeemed   *Magna et mirabilia*
Revelation 15:3-4

O ruler of the universe, Lord God,
great deeds are they that you have done,*
 surpassing human understanding.

Your ways are ways of righteousness
    and truth,*
  O King of all the ages.
Who can fail to do you homage, Lord,
and sing the praises of your Name?*
  for you only are the holy One.
All nations will draw near and fall down
    before you,*
  because your just and holy works
    have been revealed.
Glory to the Father, and to the Son,
  and to the Holy Spirit:*
  as it was in the beginning, is now,
    and will be for ever. Amen.

Songs 20 and 21 were written by early Christians, after the New Testament times. Song 20 is sung during the Holy Eucharist, so we are already familiar with it. The words of this song are similar to the words of the angels as they spoke to shepherds in the fields when Jesus was born. Songs 20 and 21 are two of the greatest Christian songs ever written.

20 Glory to God   *Gloria in excelsis*

Glory to God in the highest,
  and peace to his people on earth.
Lord God, heavenly King,
almighty God and Father,
  we worship you, we give you thanks,
  we praise you for your glory.
Lord Jesus Christ, only Son of the Father,
Lord God, Lamb of God,
you take away the sin of the world;
  have mercy on us;

you are seated at the right hand
    of the Father;
receive our prayer.

For you alone are the Holy One,
you alone are the Lord,
you alone are the Most High,
    Jesus Christ,
    with the Holy Spirit,
    in the glory of God the Father. Amen.

Song 21 was written over 1600 years ago, probably by a bishop who lived where Yugoslavia is today.

21 You are God   *Te Deum laudamus*

You are God: we praise you;
You are the Lord: we acclaim you;
You are the eternal Father:
All creation worships you.
To you all angels, all the powers of heaven,
Cherubim and Seraphim,
    sing in endless praise:
  Holy, holy, holy Lord, God of
    power and might,
  heaven and earth are full of your glory.
The glorious company of apostles praise you.
The noble fellowship of prophets praise you.
The white-robed army of martyrs praise you.
Throughout the world the holy Church
    acclaims you;
  Father, of majesty unbounded,
  your true and only Son, worthy
    of all worship,
  and the Holy Spirit, advocate and guide.
You, Christ, are the king of glory,
the eternal Son of the Father.

When you became man to set us free
you did not shun the Virgin's womb.
You overcame the sting of death
and opened the kingdom of heaven
    to all believers.
You are seated at God's right hand in glory.
We believe that you will come and be
    our judge.
    Come then, Lord, and help your people,
    bought with the price of your own blood,
    and bring us with your saints
    to glory everlasting.

The Apostles' Creed

After two or three lessons and songs, the second part of Morning Prayer ends with the Apostles' Creed. This was the creed said for us when we were baptized. When we say it now, think about what it means to belong to God's family and to be loved by God.

    Officiant and People together, all standing

I believe in God, the Father almighty,
    creator of heaven and earth.
I believe in Jesus Christ, his only Son,
    our Lord.
    He was conceived by the power
        of the Holy Spirit
        and born of the Virgin Mary.
    He suffered under Pontius Pilate,
        was crucified, died, and was buried.
    He descended to the dead.
    On the third day he rose again.
    He ascended into heaven,
        and is seated at the right hand
        of the Father.

> He will come again to judge the living
> and the dead.
> I believe in the Holy Spirit,
> the holy catholic Church,
> the communion of saints,
> the forgiveness of sins,
> the resurrection of the body,
> and the life everlasting. Amen.

The Prayers

Praying is talking with God. In the first and second parts of Morning Prayer we felt how much God loves us. So now, after learning that he loves us, we want to talk with him. For this third part of Morning Prayer we say the same prayers that were said by the early Christians in the wilderness.

> *The people stand or kneel*
>
> *Officiant* The Lord be with you.
> *People* And also with you.
> *Officiant* Let us pray.
>
> *Officiant and People*
>
> Our Father, who art in heaven,
> hallowed be thy Name,
> thy kingdom come,
> thy will be done,
> on earth as it is in heaven.
> Give us this day our daily bread.
> And forgive us our trespasses,
> as we forgive those
> who trespass against us.
> And lead us not into temptation,
> but deliver us from evil.
> For thine is the kingdom,
> and the power, and the glory,
> for ever and ever. Amen.

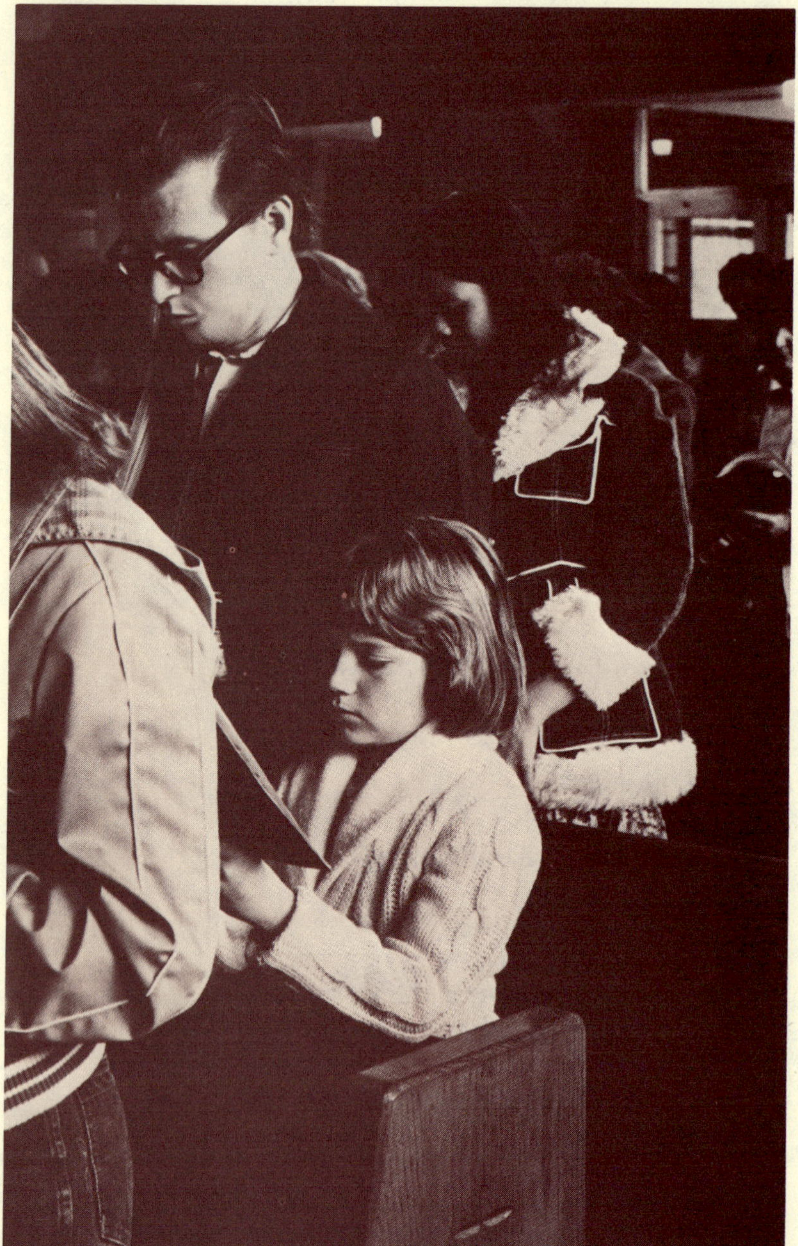

or the following

Our Father in heaven,
   hallowed be your Name,
   your kingdom come,
   your will be done,
     on earth as in heaven.
Give us today our daily bread.
Forgive us our sins
   as we forgive those
     who sin against us.
Save us from the time of trial,
   and deliver us from evil.
For the kingdom, the power,
   and the glory are yours,
     now and for ever. Amen.

The Suffrages

A suffrage is a prayer that asks for something. There are two sets of suffrages here, A and B. The leader chooses one of them. Your response is marked with an **R** at the beginning of the line. You will need to follow carefully.

Set A

V. Show us your mercy, O Lord;
R. And grant us your salvation.
V. Clothe your ministers with
   righteousness;
R. Let your people sing with joy.
V. Give peace, O Lord, in all the world;
R. For only in you can we live in safety.
V. Lord, keep this nation under
   your care:
R. And guide us in the way of justice
   and truth.
V. Let your way be known upon earth;

R. Your saving health among all nations.
V. Let not the needy, O Lord,
   be forgotten;
R. Nor the hope of the poor be taken away.
V. Create in us clean hearts, O God;
R. And sustain us with your Holy Spirit.

Set B

V. Save your people, Lord, and bless
   your inheritance;
R. Govern and uphold them,
   now and always.
V. Day by day we bless you;
R. We praise your Name for ever.
V. Lord, keep us from all sin today;
R. Have mercy on us, Lord, have mercy.
V. Lord, show us your love and mercy;
R. For we put our trust in you.
V. In you, Lord, is our hope;
R. And we shall never hope in vain.

The Collects

A collect is a very short prayer that sums up our thoughts and offers them to God. The Church has special collects for special days and for the seasons of the church calendar. One of these is called the Collect of the Day. The leader may use the Collect of the Day or one or more of the collects which are printed here. One collect will always be said for the family of God and for all people.

A Collect for Sundays

O God, you make us glad with the weekly remembrance of the glorious resurrection of your Son our Lord: Give us this day such blessing through our worship of you, that the week to come may be spent in your favor; through Jesus Christ our Lord. *Amen.*

A Collect for Fridays

Almighty God, whose most dear Son went not up to joy but first he suffered pain, and entered not into glory before he was crucified: Mercifully grant that we, walking in the way of the cross, may find it none other than the way of life and peace; through Jesus Christ your Son our Lord. *Amen.*

A Collect for Saturdays

Almighty God, who after the creation of the world rested from all your works and sanctified a day of rest for all your creatures: Grant that we, putting away all earthly anxieties, may be duly prepared for the service of your sanctuary, and that our rest here upon earth may be a preparation for the eternal rest promised to your people in heaven; through Jesus Christ our Lord. *Amen.*

A Collect for the Renewal of Life

O God, the King eternal, whose light divides the day from the night and turns the shadow of death into the morning: Drive far from us all wrong desires, incline our hearts to keep your law, and guide our feet into the way of peace; that, having done your will with cheerfulness during the day, we may, when night comes, rejoice to give you thanks; through Jesus Christ our Lord. *Amen.*

A Collect for Peace

O God, the author of peace and lover of concord, to know you is eternal life and to serve you is perfect freedom: Defend us, your humble servants, in all assaults of our enemies; that we, surely trusting in your defense, may not fear the power of any adversaries; through the might of Jesus Christ our Lord. *Amen.*

A Collect for Grace

Lord God, almighty and everlasting Father, you have brought us in safety to this new day: Preserve us with your mighty power, that we may not fall into sin, nor be overcome by adversity; and in all we do, direct us to the fulfilling of your purpose; through Jesus Christ our Lord. *Amen.*

A Collect for Guidance

Heavenly Father, in you we live and move and have our being: We humbly pray you so to guide and govern us by your Holy Spirit, that in all the cares and occupations of our life we may not forget you, but may remember that we are ever walking in your sight; through Jesus Christ our Lord. *Amen.*

Then, unless the Eucharist or a form of general intercession is to follow, one of these prayers for mission is added

Almighty and everlasting God, by whose Spirit the whole body of your faithful people is governed and sanctified: Receive our supplications and prayers which we offer before you for all members of your holy Church, that in their vocation and ministry they may truly and devoutly serve you; through our Lord and Savior Jesus Christ. *Amen.*

or this

O God, you have made of one blood all the peoples of the earth, and sent your blessed Son to preach peace to those who are far off and to those who are near: Grant that people everywhere may seek after you and find you; bring the nations into your fold; pour out your Spirit upon all flesh; and hasten the coming of your kingdom; through Jesus Christ our Lord. *Amen.*

or the following

Lord Jesus Christ, you stretched out your arms of love on the hard wood of the cross that everyone might come within the reach of your saving embrace: So clothe us in your Spirit that we, reaching forth our hands in love, may bring those who do not know you to the knowledge and love of you; for the honor of your Name. *Amen.*

This part of Morning Prayer often ends with a song. As this service has become more popular, requests for God's blessing and thanksgiving have also been added to the ending.

The General Thanksgiving

Officiant and People

Almighty God, Father of all mercies,
we your unworthy servants give you
    humble thanks
for all your goodness and loving-kindness
to us and to all whom you have made.
We bless you for our creation, preservation,
and all the blessings of this life;
but above all for your immeasurable love
in the redemption of the world by our
    Lord Jesus Christ;
for the means of grace, and for the
    hope of glory.
And, we pray, give us such an awareness
    of your mercies,
that with truly thankful hearts we may
    show forth your praise,

not only with our lips, but in our lives,
by giving up our selves to your service,
and by walking before you
in holiness and righteousness all our days;
through Jesus Christ our Lord,
to whom, with you and the Holy Spirit,
be honor and glory throughout all ages.
Amen.

The Ending

The service comes to a close with a prayer written by a bishop named John. This bishop was so good at preaching that he had the title *Chrysostom,* which means *golden-mouthed.*. Saint Chrysostom lived a very long time ago. His prayer tells us that Jesus promised to be with us whenever we gather together to remember him.

A Prayer of St. Chrysostom

Almighty God, you have given us grace at this time with one accord to make our common supplication to you; and you have promised through your well-beloved Son that when two or three are gathered together in his Name you will be in the midst of them: Fulfill now, O Lord, our desires and petitions as may be best for us; granting us in this world knowledge of your truth, and in the age to come life everlasting. *Amen.*

Then may be said
Let us bless the Lord.
Thanks be to God.

From Easter Day through the Day of Pentecost "Alleluia, alleluia" may be added to the preceding versicle and response.

The Officiant may then conclude with one of the following

The grace of our Lord Jesus Christ, and the love of God, and the fellowship of the Holy Spirit, be with us all evermore. *Amen.*   *2 Corinthians 13:14*

May the God of hope fill us with all joy and peace in believing through the power of the Holy Spirit. *Amen.*   *Romans 15:13*

Glory to God whose power, working in us, can do infinitely more than we can ask or imagine: Glory to him from generation to generation in the Church, and in Christ Jesus for ever and ever. *Amen.*   *Ephesians 3:20, 21*

Daily Prayers for Individuals and Families

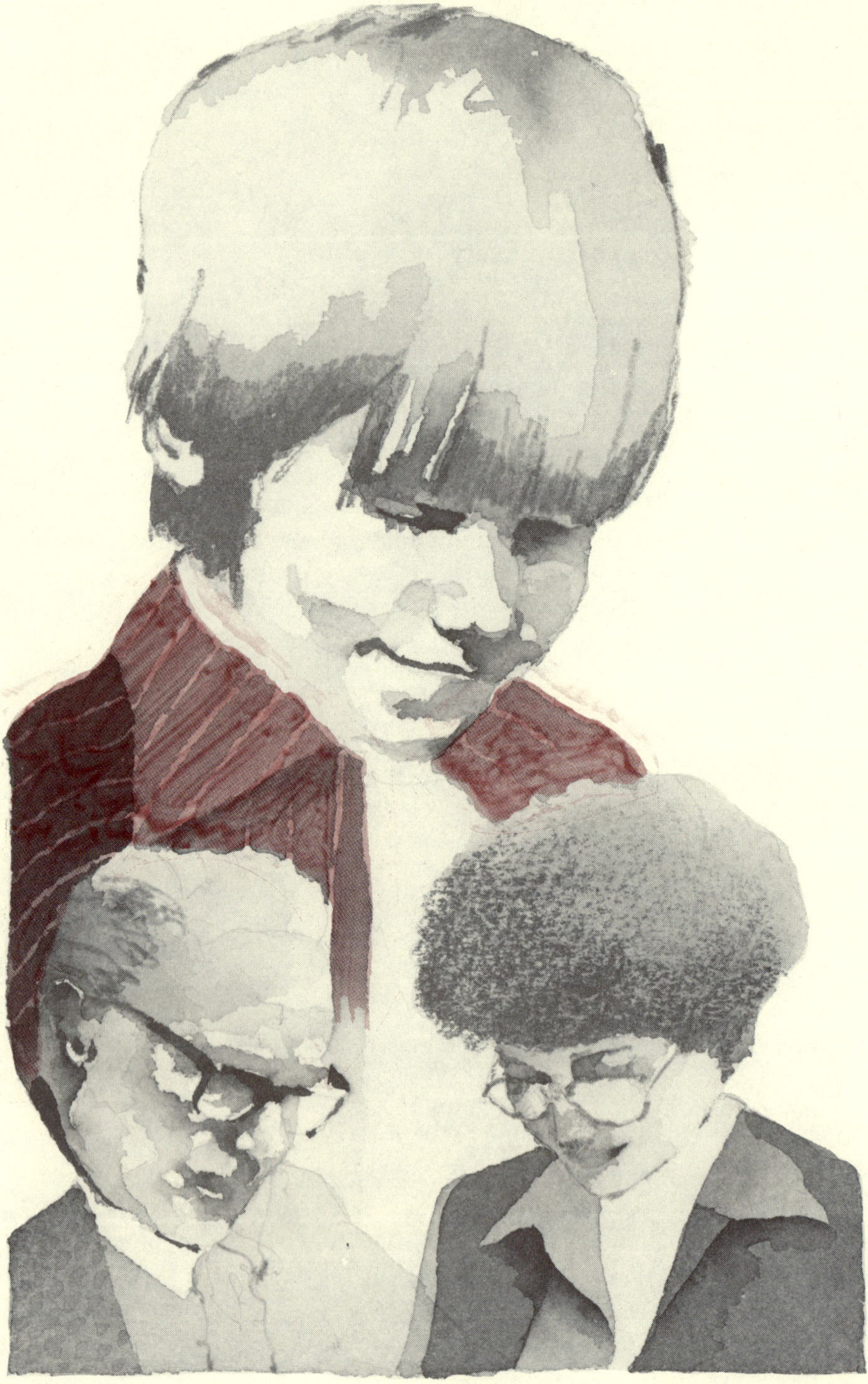

Up to this point everything in this prayer book has described what we do in the church with other members of the family of God. But some of the most important moments with God happen in our own families. Your home is a place where you gather with your parents and your sisters and brothers. Christians have always worshiped together with their own families as well as in the church family.

Sometimes you do this at mealtimes or just before you go to bed. This kind of worship doesn't have to take long. But however long it takes, it's a time to come together and to welcome God's presence in your family. It's a time to think about what God says to us.

The Church year has a place in family worship. Your parish priest can help your family find special home rituals to remind you of the meaning of Advent, Christmas, Epiphany, Lent, Easter, and Pentecost.

Everybody in your family can take part in the short periods of prayer and praise that are presented in this section of your prayer book. Ask your mother or father to use these prayers and readings at your meals or before you go to bed. You can all take turns reading them out loud.

Morning

At the beginning of each day we want to remember that God will be here with us, helping us all day.

From Psalm 51

Open my lips, O Lord,*
   and my mouth shall proclaim
      your praise.
Create in me a clean heart, O God,*
   and renew a right spirit within me.
Cast me not away from your presence*
   and take not your holy Spirit from me.
Give me the joy of your saving help again*
   and sustain me with your
      bountiful Spirit.
Glory to the Father, and to the Son,
   and to the Holy Spirit:*
   as it was in the beginning, is now,
      and will be for ever. Amen.

A Reading

Blessed be the God and Father of our Lord Jesus Christ! By his great mercy we have been born anew to a living hope through the resurrection of Jesus Christ from the dead.   *1 Peter 1:3*

A period of silence may follow.

A hymn or canticle may be used; the Apostles' Creed may be said.

Prayers may be offered for ourselves and others.

The Lord's Prayer

Praying with the Family of God

The Collect

Lord God, almighty and everlasting Father, you have brought us in safety to this new day: Preserve us with your mighty power, that we may not fall into sin, nor be overcome by adversity; and in all we do, direct us to the fulfilling of your purpose; through Jesus Christ our Lord. *Amen.*

Noon

At noon we think of the peace that God gives through the love of Jesus.

From Psalm 113

Give praise, you servants of the Lord:*
    praise the Name of the Lord.
Let the Name of the Lord be blessed,*
    from this time forth for evermore.
From the rising of the sun to its
    going down*
    let the Name of the Lord be praised.
The Lord is high above all nations,*
    and his glory above the heavens.

A Reading

O God, you will keep in perfect peace those whose minds are fixed on you; for in returning and rest we shall be saved; in quietness and trust shall be our strength. *Isaiah 26:3; 30:15*

Prayers may be offered for ourselves and others.

The Lord's Prayer

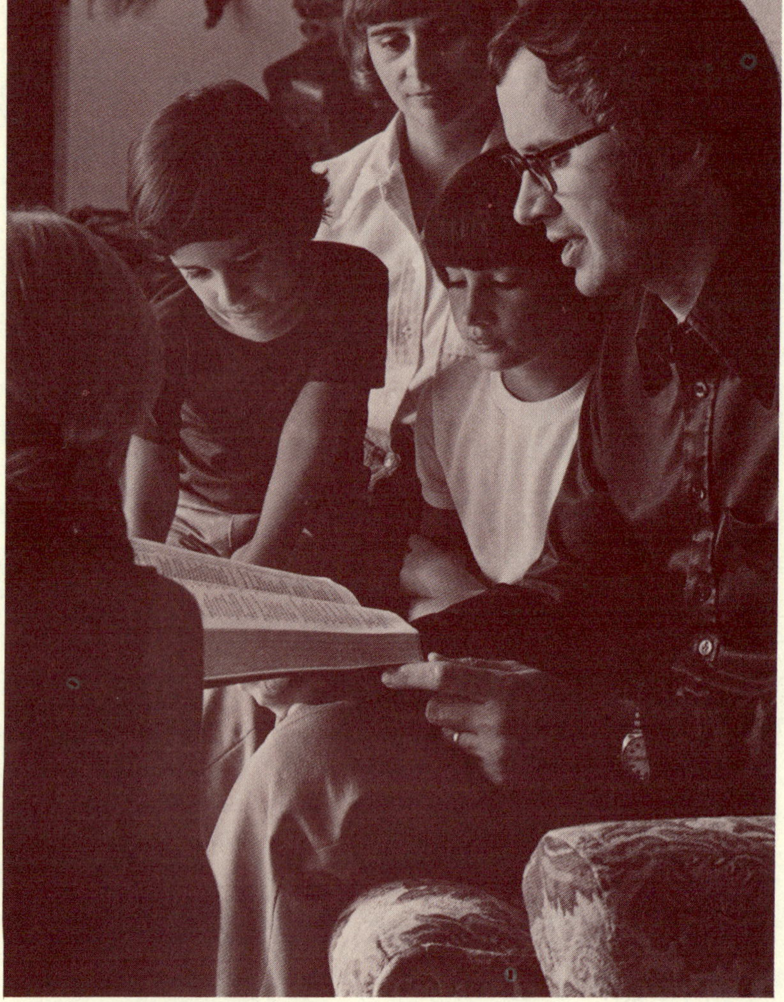

The Collect

Blessed Savior, at this hour you hung upon the cross, stretching out your loving arms: Grant that all the peoples of the earth may look to you and be saved; for your mercies' sake. *Amen.*

or this

Lord Jesus Christ, you said to your apostles, "Peace I give to you; my own peace I leave with you:" Regard not our sins, but the faith of your Church, and give to us the peace and unity of that heavenly City, where with the Father and the Holy Spirit you live and reign, now and for ever. *Amen.*

Early Evening

We ask Jesus to shine light into the darkness of our lives, and we ask him to help us make his light known everywhere in the world. This prayer may be used before or after the evening meal. Or you may use the Order of Worship for the Evening, in *The Book of Common Prayer.*

> O gracious Light,
> pure brightness of the everliving Father
>   in heaven,
> O Jesus Christ, holy and blessed!
> Now as we come to the setting of the sun,
> and our eyes behold the vesper light,
> we sing your praises O God: Father,
>   Son, and Holy Spirit.
> You are worthy at all times to be praised
>   by happy voices,
> O Son of God, O Giver of life,
> and to be glorified through all the worlds.

A Reading

It is not ourselves that we proclaim; we proclaim Christ Jesus as Lord, and ourselves as your servants, for Jesus' sake. For the same God who said, "Out of darkness let light shine," has caused his light to shine within us, to give the light of revelation—the revelation of the glory of God in the face of Jesus Christ.   *2 Corinthians 4:5-6*

Prayers may be offered for ourselves and others.

The Lord's Prayer

The Collect

Lord Jesus, stay with us, for evening is at hand and the day is past; be our companion in the way, kindle our hearts, and awaken hope, that we may know you as you are revealed in Scripture and the breaking of bread. Grant this for the sake of your love. *Amen.*

Close of the Day

We ask God to bless our home and to be with us while we sleep.

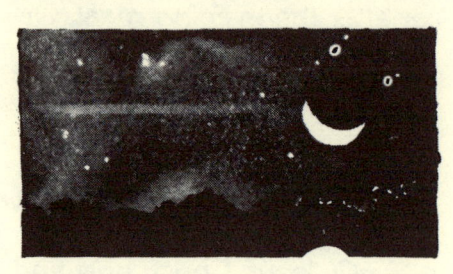

Psalm 134

Behold now, bless the Lord,
    all you servants of the Lord,*
  you that stand by night in the house
    of the Lord.
Lift up your hands in the holy place
    and bless the Lord;*
  the Lord who made heaven and
    earth bless you out of Zion.

A Reading

Lord, you are in the midst of us and we are called by your Name: Do not forsake us, O Lord our God. *Jeremiah 14:9, 22*

The following may be said

Lord, you now have set your servant free*
   to go in peace as you have promised;
For these eyes of mine have seen
     the Savior*
   whom you have prepared for all the
     world to see:
A Light to enlighten the nations,*
   and the glory of your people Israel.

We may also include additional prayers for ourselves and others, prayers of thanksgiving for the blessings of the day, and prayers asking forgiveness.

The Lord's Prayer

The Collect

Visit this place, O Lord, and drive far from it all snares of the enemy; let your holy angels dwell with us to preserve us in peace; and let your blessing be upon us always; through Jesus Christ our Lord. *Amen.*

The almighty and merciful Lord, Father, Son, and Holy Spirit, bless us and keep us. *Amen.*

Glossary

Absolution
A prayer in which the priest assures us that God forgives us. This is done after we have confessed our sins. A priest has the power to declare the absolution of our sins in God's name.

Anthem
A sacred song that two groups of people sing back and forth to each other. Sometimes everyone sings together.

Antiphon
A single sentence which is said or sung by the congregation at the end of a psalm and sometimes at breaks during the psalm.

Canticle
A liturgical song that comes from the Bible.

Celebrant
The priest who leads Holy Baptism or Holy Eucharist. From its earliest days the Church has required that certain sacramental rites be done by people with special training and preparation. That person is usually a priest.

Chancel
Where the altar is. The chancel also has a pulpit or reading desk. The clergy and their assistants sit in the chancel. Often the choir sits there too. In some churches the part of the chancel where the altar stands is called the sanctuary. (The area people sit in is called the nave.)

Chrism
The oil used to mark (anoint) people being baptized. From a Greek word meaning *to anoint.*

Collect

A brief prayer which sums up or "collects" a particular thought or an idea we especially want to share with God on a given day or on a special occasion.

Consecration

To consecrate something means *to make it special,* to change it for God's purpose. In Christian worship the consecration is a prayer which sets the bread and wine apart as the Body and Blood of Jesus.

Covenant

An agreement between two or more people. A promise. In the Christian religion there is the *old covenant* between God and the Hebrews and the *new covenant* between God and those who have faith in him through Jesus.

Creed

A statement of belief. The word *creed* comes from a Latin word which means *put your trust in someone.* Our creed says that we trust God and we know he cares for us.

Doxology

A statement of praise to God: "Glory to the Father, and to the Son, and to the Holy Spirit; as it was in the beginning, is now, and will be for ever. Amen." Sometimes called the *Gloria Patri.*

Epistle

A letter. *Epistle* comes from a Greek word meaning *letter.* In the New Testament an epistle is usually a letter written by Saint Paul to a group of new Christians. The letter contains advice on problems faced by the new Church. When we listen to the epistle, we are hearing one of these letters.

Eucharist
In Greek this word means *thanksgiving*. In the Holy Eucharist we give thanks for the death and resurrection of Jesus. We also call this the Holy Thanksgiving.

Gospel
Gospel means the *good news*. Four books in the New Testament tell us the good news of Jesus. We call them the four Gospels. In our service a reading from any one of these four books is called the Gospel.

Holy Communion
The part of the Eucharist where we eat and drink the Body and Blood of Christ in order to be together with God and one another as a family. The word *communion* means *to be together,* like a family is together.

Intercession
A prayer that asks for something. If you pray to God to heal your sister, that is an intercession.

Invitatory Psalm
A psalm that calls us to worship. Psalm 95 was first used as an invitatory psalm 1300 years ago.

Invocation
A prayer in which we call on God for his blessing.

Litany
A prayer in which the leader makes a short request to God, and then the congregation responds. Then the leader makes another request, and again the congregation responds. This is sometimes called *call and response.*

Liturgy
Our worship rituals. The services we join in at church.

Sometimes the liturgy means the Holy Eucharist. Its name comes from a Greek word that means *the work of the people.*

Maundy Thursday

The day on which Jesus gave us a new commandment to love one another as he loves us. *Maundy* comes from a Latin word that means *commandment.*

Offertory

The portion of the service in which we offer gifts to God. Our gifts are bread and wine or money for the support of the church.

Paschal Candle

The candle that burns from Easter until Ascension Thursday. Its name comes from a Jewish word meaning *passover,* because Easter celebrates the time Jesus "passed over" from death to life.

The Peace

The moment in our service when members of the congregation share peace with each other by exchanging a kiss or shaking hands. Sometimes we simply hug or greet one another with words of God's peace.

The Prayers of the People

The prayers in the Holy Eucharist that come after the creed. From ancient times Christians have taken this time in the Eucharist to talk to God about what is on their minds.

Psalm

A poem from the Old Testament which was sung to the accompaniment of a stringed instrument. There are 150 psalms in the Old Testament.

Sacrament

A religious act which tells part of the story of the family of God and which brings us closer to God. Baptism and Holy Eucharist are two of the church's sacraments.

Sermon

The part of the service when the priest or someone appointed by the priest talks with the people about what the Bible readings mean for our lives today. *Sermon* means *conversation* in Latin.

Suffrage

A prayer that asks God for something. A petition. An intercession.

Versicle

A short sentence said by the priest and responded to by the congregation. The versicle often asks God for something.